AFRICA: FINANCIAL SECTORS

A Guide to the Financial Infrastructure of Sub-Saharan Africa

by
Paula Mitchell
Trade Development, Office of Finance

U.S. DEPARTMENT OF COMMERCE
International Trade Administration
Washington, D.C.: 2001

Library of Congress Cataloging-in-Publication Statement

Mitchell, Paula.
  Africa : financial sectors : a guide to the financial infrastructure of
sub-Saharan Africa / by Paula Mitchell.
    p.   cm.
  1. Finance—Africa, Sub-Saharan. 2. Financial institutions—Africa,
Sub-Saharan—Commerce. I. Title.

HG187.5.A357 M58 2001
332'.0967—dc21

                                                                    2001039558

FOREWORD

Africa has always been seen as a difficult financial market because of its countries' political and economic problems. Today, however, market liberalization conditions are making the continent increasingly attractive to foreign traders and investors. Direct investments by the United States in Africa returned an impressive 19 percent on book value from 1997 to 2000, compared with an average 10 percent return for such investments elsewhere. Private investments in Africa are projected to continue to grow, rising in proportion from the current level of less than 10 percent of investment flows to developing countries as a group.

Many African countries now have democratically elected governments. Africa has also made slow but steady progress in liberalizing its markets by introducing market-oriented reforms, entering into regional cooperation agreements that facilitate trade, and taking steps toward currency convertibility. Currency convertibility has long been a problem for investors wanting to do business in Africa, but the situation has improved since the International Monetary Fund and the World Bank recommended in 1986 that African nations make their currencies convertible.

Financial sectors are expected to play an essential and critical role in the economic growth and development of the continent. Some African countries have made great strides in implementing gradual market reforms intended to improve their financial systems. The financial systems in most African countries are still, however, undercapitalized, underdeveloped, and in need of restructuring.

This publication, which profiles financial sectors in 28 sub-Saharan African countries, was prepared to assist U.S. companies interested in engaging in trade with Africa. The prime criterion for inclusion in this report was that the country have a substantial, functioning financial services infrastructure. The information and analysis provided reflect information current as of July 2001.

While reforms have not eliminated many cultural and commercial problems that affect the conduct of business in Africa, opportunities await U.S. companies that are prepared to enter the region's markets for the long term.

While every effort has been made to ensure the accuracy of the information presented in this report, U.S. exporters considering business opportunities in sub-Saharan Africa should conduct their own due diligence.

For their assistance in the compilation of this study, the author wishes to extend her thanks to the embassies of the countries profiled.

CONTENTS

V

Acronyms and Abbreviations

BCEAO   Banque Centrale des Etats de l'Afrique de l'Ouest (Central Bank of West African States; member states are Benin, Burkina Faso, Ivory Coast, Guinea-Bissau, Mali, Niger, Senegal, and Togo)

BEAC   Banque Centrale des Etats d'Afrique Centrale (Bank of Central African States; member states are Cameroon, Central African Republic, Chad, the Republic of Congo, Equatorial Guinea, and Gabon)

BRVM   Bourse Régionale des Valeurs Mobilières (West African Regional Stock Exchange)

CDC   Commonwealth Development Corporation

CEMAC   Communauté Economique et Monétaire de l'Afrique Centrale (Central African Economic and Monetary Community)

CFA   Communauté Financière Africaine (African Financial Community)

CIMA   Conférence Interafricaine des Marchés d'Assurances (Interafrican Conference of Insurance Markets)

ECOWAS   Economic Community of West African States

GDP   gross domestic product

IMF   International Monetary Fund

MIGA   Multilateral Investment Guarantee Agency

NGO   nongovernmental organization

OPIC   Overseas Private Investment Corporation

UDEAC   Union Douanière des Etats de l'Afrique Centrale (Customs Union of Central African States)

WAEMU   West African Economic and Monetary Union (also known by its French acronym UEMOA; member states include Benin, Burkina Faso, Ivory Coast, Guinea-Bissau, Mali, Niger, Senegal, and Togo)

Note: Throughout the text, many figures in local currencies have been converted to dollar equivalents. Unless otherwise noted, these represent U.S. dollars calculated at exchange rates current as of mid-2001.

Banking Infrastructure

Angola's banking system consists of the central bank, the National Bank of Angola, two state-owned commercial banks, two local banks with foreign shareholdings, and three Portuguese banks.

The two state-owned commercial banks, Banco de Poupança e Crédito and Banco de Comércio e Industria, are being assessed for eventual privatization, in accordance with the Financial Sector Assessment Program, a joint IMF and World Bank program.

The two local banks with foreign shareholdings are the Banco Angolano de Investimento and the Bank of Angola. The three privately owned Portuguese banks are the Banco Portugues do Atlantico, Banco de Fomento e Exterior, and Banco Totta e Açores.

In accordance with Angola's financial institutions law, foreign-owned banks are obliged to observe Angolan laws and regulations. Authorization to operate as a financial institution must be recommended by the National Bank of Angola and approved by the Council of Ministers.

Lack of access to financing is one of the most frequently heard complaints of Angolan business representatives. General financing is not readily available to local Angolan companies. Real interest rates on Kwanza-denominated transactions remain negative in spite of interest rate liberalization. Most banks are not equipped to carry out serious credit analysis on potential borrowers. Asset-backed collateralization of loans is not provided for under current Angolan law.

Citibank and Equator Bank currently have representative offices in Luanda.

Stock Market

At present, Angola does not have a stock market. However, detailed technical studies on the subject have been presented to the Angolan government for consideration.

Insurance Industry

The insurance industry has not yet been privatized, but legislation authorizing the privatization of this industry has been approved by Parliament. Information on this industry is not available.

Other Finance Programs

The U.S. Export-Import Bank carries out financial operations supporting American companies doing business in the Angolan petroleum sector. These transactions are permitted as limited recourse financing, guaranteed by funds deposited in the London-based Cabinda Trust.

OPIC, a U.S. government agency, and the U.S. Trade Development Agency are authorized to support American firms pursuing business interests in Angola through loans, risk insurance, and funded feasibility studies. Angola is a member of MIGA.

U.S. Department of Commerce, International Trade Administration

BENIN

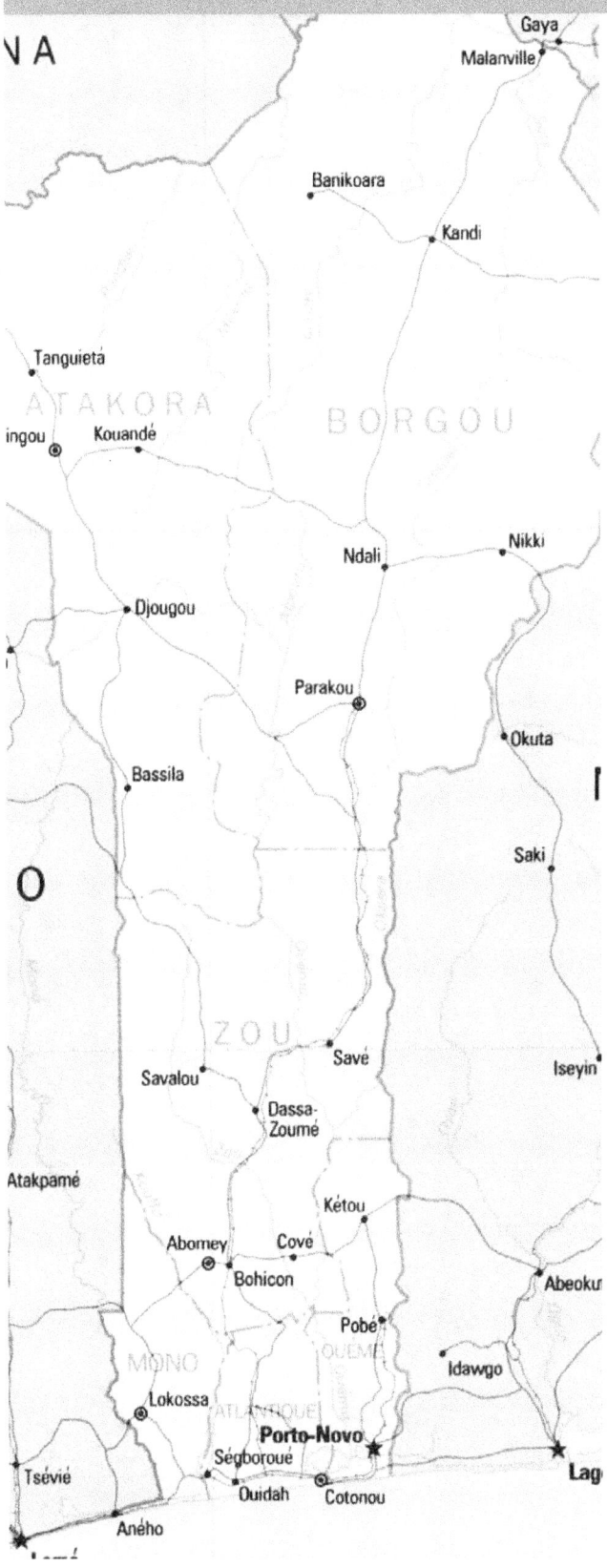

Banking Infrastructure

Benin's banking system is governed by the BCEAO. Benin, along with seven other franc zone nations, is a member of the WAEMU. Other member countries are Burkina Faso, Guinea-Bissau, the Ivory Coast, Mali, Niger, Senegal, and Togo.

WAEMU established BCEAO, which issued the CFA franc, the unit of currency for the member states, and established policies governing interest rates. BCEAO banking supervision, strengthened by the role of the WAEMU Banking Commission, has enhanced the enforcement and regulatory provisions of the banking system. BCEAO also has the power to monitor other financial institutions. It is closely monitored by the French treasury.

The banking system was state owned between 1974 and 1988, and finally failed at the end of that period because of mismanagement and a serious liquidity crisis. Private deposits were frozen and assets of commercial banks blocked. By the end of 1988, no commercial banks were functioning in the country. With assistance and guidelines from the World Bank and the IMF, the state took appropriate measures to attract foreign banks back to Benin beginning in 1989. Several commercial banks are now operating in the country.

Other financial systems include Crédit Promotion Benin, postal checking accounts, the savings bank, and Sonar, a state-owned insurance company.

Local Banks. Local banks are able to provide general financing services, with specific terms varying by bank. Interest rates are considered high. While the local business community would like the existing banks to grant them more credit and financing for the creation of small and medium-sized enterprises, the banks are reluctant to loan to firms without a proven record.

Commercial Banks. Commercial bank services are

open to small bearers and have several branches operating in the main cities. Several banks offer letters of credit. Some commercial banks have correspondent banking arrangements with U. S. banks. Opened in January 1990, the Bank of Africa, which has correspondent arrangements with U.S. banks, is estimated to have approximately 4 percent of the market. The majority of shareholders are Beninese.

Foreign Banks. Created in 1990 on the initiative of businesspeople from the 16 ECOWAS countries and the Federation of West African Chambers of Commerce, Ecobank-US operates freely in Benin. It is a limited liability company with a capital of 1 billion CFA francs. It offers the full range of traditional banking services and is committed to playing an important part in improving and refining banking systems and procedures to meet international standards. Its activities are focused on the economic development of Benin in particular and on the promotion of investment opportunities in the sub-region of West Africa.

Financing is also available from a private joint venture, Banque Internationale du Benin, created in 1990 by four major Nigerian banks (Union Bank of Nigeria PLC, First Bank of Nigeria, Continental Merchant Bank, and First Interstate Merchant Bank) in collaboration with private investors from Benin and Nigeria. The bank has helped to improve trade and investments between Benin and Nigeria and between Benin and other countries. Other foreign and U.S. banks that offer financing in Benin are Citibank, Midland Bank, Financial Bank, American Express Bank Ltd., Bankers Trust New York, and Crédit Lyonnais.

Other foreign financial organizations that offer development finances for Benin trade and projects are the African Development Bank, West African Bank for Development, European Development Fund, Caisse Centrale de Cooperation Economique, Proparco, International Fund for Economic Development, and the Islamic Bank of African Economic Development.

Stock Market

Benin is a member of the Bourse Régionale des Valeurs Mobilières, a regional stock market located in Abidjan, Ivory Coast. Established in 1996, this regional stock market became effective in the last three months of 1998. This exchange links Benin with the other French-speaking member countries of the West African Economic and Monetary Union: Burkina Faso, Guinea-Bissau, Ivory Coast, Mali, Niger, Senegal, and Togo.

Insurance Industry

The insurance industry in Benin, which was established during the colonial period, consists of nine operating insurance companies. The types of insurance available are maritime and air transport, fire, home owners, industrial hazards, comprehensive or occupational third-party liability, life, personal injury, accident, medical, and various risks.

While the insurance companies are Beninese-owned, some are joint ventures with West African and French businesses. No insurance company is wholly foreign-owned.

Other Finance Programs

The U.S. Export-Import Bank is only available for short- and medium-term financing. Benin is a member of MIGA, and OPIC programs are available.

BOTSWANA

Banking Infrastructure

The central bank, the Bank of Botswana, regulates the banking sector and other financial institutions operating in Botswana. Established in 1975, it is responsible for the management of Botswana's monetary policies and its substantial foreign exchange reserves. The central bank is also responsible for processing applications, issuing banking licences, and monitoring the banking sector's performance and compliance, capital adequacy, asset quality, and liquidity requirements.

In his 1999 budget speech, the minister of finance and development planning announced that the government was taking steps to promote Botswana as a financial service center for southern Africa, a step that has moved the country toward liberalization, including the complete abolition of all exchange controls on February 8, 1999. To achieve this goal, the government hired an international consulting firm to review all statutory, fiscal, and regulatory structures in the financial sector, with a view toward liberalization.

No U.S. financial lending institutions or multilateral development banks currently operate in the country.

Commercial Banks. Four major commercial banks operate in Botswana: Barclays Bank of Botswana, Ltd., Standard Chartered Bank of Botswana, Ltd., First National Bank of Botswana, Ltd., and Stanbic Bank Botswana, Ltd. All four have correspondent relationships with U.S. banks.

At present, commercial banks finance only about one-third of the annual investment taking place in Botswana. Short-term financing, including pre- and post-shipment credit, is readily available through the commercial banking system at market rates of interest. However, banks have been hampered from making long-term credit available by the short maturity of their deposits and small capital bases.

As of February 8, 1999, restrictions on the amount

of funds that foreign investors can lend to nonresident-controlled entities have been completely removed. The provisions for U.S. and other foreign firms borrowing in Botswana are liberal. Commercial banks are authorized to open foreign currency accounts for residents, temporary residents, and nonresidents without restriction. Between February 17, 1997, and February 24, 1998, commercial banks were allowed to open foreign currency accounts in any currency at their discretion, up to the equivalent of 1 million pula for individuals and 10 million pula for companies. On February 25, 1998, the restriction was removed, and commercial banks were authorized to open foreign currency accounts for their customers for any amount in any currency at the discretion of banks. Nonresidents are permitted to open pula accounts in Botswana without prior approval from the Bank of Botswana.

Development Banks. Botswana has established development financial institutions that supplement the role of commercial banks, offering specialized services and long-term investment financing targeted at certain economic sectors and activities. Two of the institutions, both autonomous Botswana government agencies, are the National Development Bank and the Botswana Development Corporation. Both foreign and domestic investors are equally eligible for loans from both banks.

Investment Banks. In 1998, a new private investment bank, Investec Bank (Botswana) was licensed. Its primary goal is to fill the gap that currently exists in long-term investment lending by commercial banks. Investec Bank will provide investment and merchant banking services including underwriting and brokerage, financial solutions to selected market problems, investment advisory services, select deposit taking, and trade finance.

Stock Market

The Botswana Stock Exchange, a small but thriving exchange, began in June 1989 when the Botswana Development Corporation needed a vehicle to sell its investments. Presently, the exchange has 14 publicly held companies.

Between 1989 and 1995, the listing rules, member rules, and all general requirements used in the market were developed in cooperation with the Zimbabwe Stock Exchange. At that time, the exchange had no legal status, as Botswana did not have a Stock Exchange Act. In 1994 the government instituted an interim Stock Exchange Committee comprised of representatives of the exchange and the Ministry of Finance to formalize the exchange's existence and its legal requirements. The exchange became a legal entity on November 1, 1995, after Parliament passed the Botswana Stock Exchange Act in August 1994. The exchange is a member of the Committee of the South African Development Community Stock Exchange, which is working to harmonize stock exchange regulations throughout the region in accordance with recommendations by the Organization for Economic Cooperation and Development.

Limited foreign investment and foreign ownership are permitted in the Botswana Stock Exchange. No one foreigner may own more than 10 percent of the issued capital of a publicly quoted company, and foreign ownership of the free stock of a local company trading on the exchange may not exceed 55 percent.

The Botswana Stock Exchange also trades nine dual-listed companies, including De Beers, Morgan Stanley Fund Africa, Avis Holdings, and McCarthy Retail. Dual listing has only been possible since the liberalization of exchange controls in early 1997. All listings are presently included in the only index, the Botswana Share Market Index, which is weighted according to the volume of shares in issue and the current bid price. Private investors are estimated to account for 8 percent of the total market capitalization.

The Botswana Stock Exchange also acts as the vehicle for Botswana's bond market. In December 1997, the Botswana Development Corporation floated seven-year bonds on the exchange that carried a 14 percent fixed rate of interest. Total funding from the bonds amounted to 50 million pula. The Botswana Telecommunications Corporation also floated a 50 million pula bond, which will be redeemable in 2008. Investec Overseas Finance Limited issued a floating rate note, with an authorized limit of 500 million pula, on July 22, 1998. The government is actively attempting to promote a deeper bond market and has therefore liberalized issue rules and is now allowing nonresidents to be able to hold bonds with maturity periods of over one year.

U.S. Department of Commerce, International Trade Administration

Insurance Industry

Botswana's insurance industry has grown steadily over the last few years and now consists of 10 insurance companies, 14 insurance brokers, and 40 insurance agencies. In 1997, Botswana-registered insurers and brokers invested about 779.3 million pula, of which 85.7 percent was invested in three main areas: 59.6 percent in fixed and variable interest securities and equities, 15.3 percent in deposits, and 10.8 percent in land and buildings. Long-term insurers tended to invest in land and buildings while short-term insurers concentrated their investments in deposits and cash. The total assets of Botswana's insurance industry increased by 40.7 percent between 1996 and 1997, total liabilities from 1.08 to 1.12 percent. In 1998, the industry incurred about 82.6 million pula in payments of claims, of which 69.5 percent were due to motor vehicle losses. There are no premium taxes or tariffs levied on Botswana's insurance companies.

Botswana's insurance industry is currently governed by the Insurance Industry Act of 1987, which is considered somewhat outdated. In 1999, the government began reviewing this act to reflect the changing needs of the industry and bring it in line with current insurance practices. The government has recently inaugurated an Insurance Advisory Board consisting of insurers, insurance brokers, the registrar of insurance, and other stakeholders to assist with this process.

Direct insurers, insurance brokers, and insurance agencies are regulated and monitored by the registrar of insurance located within the Ministry of Finance and Development Planning. The registrar is a member of the International Association of Insurance Supervisors. Foreign reinsurers are not required to be registered in Botswana prior to doing business with Botswana=s direct insurers. There are no locally registered reinsurers. At present, the registrar examines the following areas for each insurance company as required under current law:

- Adequacy of capital and compliance with solvency equirements,
- Rate of growth in premium income,
- Correctness of technical reserving,
- Proper management and level of control,
- Standards of underwriting and technically sound premium rates,
- Adequacy of accounting skills, and
- Currency matching for overseas liabilities.

Insurance policies are provided by Botswana Insurance Holdings, Ltd., and Botswana Eagle Insurance Company, Ltd. Export credit insurance is available through local insurance companies.

In addition to the above private insurers, the government of Botswana maintains the Government Employees Motor Vehicle Advance Scheme and the Local Authorities Scheme, which offer certain types of insurance to certain categories of civil servants. In addition, the Motor Vehicle Insurance Fund, an autonomous government agency funded from gasoline sales, handles all third-party bodily injury liability motor vehicle insurance in Botswana.

Formed in 1976, the Botswana Eagle Insurance Company, Ltd., has approximately 30 percent of the short-term insurance market in Botswana. The company is a wholly owned subsidiary of South African Eagle, which in turn is owned 58 percent by Eagle Star Holdings, U.K., and 25 percent by Anglo American Corporation, South Africa. BAT Industries is the major shareholder in Eagle Star. Botswana Eagle Star transacts only short-term insurance business.

Other Financial Programs

OPIC insurance is available to U.S. investors in Botswana. U.S. Export-Import Bank programs are available to exporters to finance exports to Botswana. The bank has not, however, been active in Botswana in recent years. Botswana is a member of MIGA.

BURKINA FASO

Banking Infrastructure

Burkina Faso's banking system is governed by the BCEAO. Burkina Faso, along with seven other franc zone nations, is a member of the WAEMU. Other member countries are Benin, Guinea-Bissau, Ivory Coast, Mali, Niger, Senegal, and Togo.

WAEMU established the BCEAO, which issued the CFA franc, the unit of currency for the member states, and established policies governing interest rates. BCEAO banking supervision, strengthened by the role of the WAEMU Banking Commission, has enhanced the enforcement and regulatory provisions of the banking system. BCEAO also has the power to monitor other financial institutions.

Burkina Faso has a relatively well-developed banking system, with six commercial banks and three specialized credit institutions called "établissements financiers." The six banks are Banque Commerciale du Burkina, Banque Internationale du Burkina, Banque Internationale du Commerce de l'Industrie et de l'Agriculture du Burkina, Bank of Africa Burkina Faso, Caisse Nationale de Crédit Agricole, and Société Generale de Banques du Burkina. The banking sector has no restrictions or discrimination against foreign investors.

The three specialized credit institutions finance the majority of home, furniture, car, and moped acquisitions: Société Burkinabe d'Equipment, Société Burkinabe de Crédit Automobile, and La Financière du Burkina.

The Banque Internationale du Burkina and the Banque Internationale du Commerce de l'Industrie et de l'Agriculture du Burkina have correspondent banks in the United States, mainly Citibank, American Express Bank, and Chase Manhattan.

Stock Market

Burkina Faso is a member of the Bourse Régionale des

Valeurs Mobilières, a regional stock market located in Abidjan, Ivory Coast. Established in 1996, this regional stock market became effective in the last three months of 1998. It links Burkina Faso with the other French-speaking member countries of the West African Economic and Monetary Union: Benin, Guinea Bissau, Ivory Coast, Mali, Niger, Senegal, and Togo. Currently, only one company from Burkina Faso, Brasserie du Burkina, is listed.

Insurance Industry

The insurance industry in Burkina Faso has been established since the colonial period. The first national company was established in 1969. The Ministry of Economy and Finance regulates the insurance industry with the assistance of a technical committee of the insurance companies. The main insurance companies are: FON-CIAS/Athena Assurances; Générale des Assurances; Société Nationale d'Assurances et de Reassurance; Sicar, Faugers et Jutheau; and Union des Assurances du Burkina.

The Société Nationale d'Assurances et de Reassurance (Sonar) was established by the government in the 1960s, but has since been restructured and privatized. The other insurers are owned by the private sector and foreign partners.

The insurance industry has no restrictions on, or discrimination for, foreign investors.

Other Financial Programs

The World Bank, the European Union, the African Development Bank, and other donors are actively engaged in Burkina Faso. Burkina Faso is eligible for OPIC programs, but there has never been OPIC involvement in an investment project in Burkina Faso. Burkina Faso is also eligible for U.S. Export-Import Bank short-term insurance and is a member of MIGA.

Banking Infrastructure

Cameroon's banking system is controlled by the BEAC, a multilateral central bank which also serves five other CEMAC countries. The other members are the Central African Republic, Chad, the Republic of Congo, Gabon, and Guinea. BEAC is closely monitored by the French Treasury.

Structuring of the financial system began in 1986 and is now considered complete and sustainable, but fragile. The ratio of provision for doubtful loans is low and much of the total asset base of the banks is estimated as non-performing. Private finance firms are free to associate with any partner they choose and in whatever percentage participation they negotiate with such partners. Finance companies are also free to organize into industry associations.

Banks may lend to nonresidents who maintain accounts with them. Foreign investors are able to obtain credit on the local market, but usually borrow offshore due to high domestic interest rates. Foreign investors continue to face high risks because Cameroon's legal and regulatory systems are inefficient and often arbitrary, and the government has not yet established a regulatory system to protect and encourage portfolio investments.

Foreign borrowing, whether public or private, requires prior authorization of the Ministry of Economy and Finance. The following, however, are exempt from this authorization and require only a report:

1. loans directly connected with the rendering of services abroad by the persons or firms whose residence or registered office is in Cameroon, or with the financing of commercial transactions either between Cameroon and countries abroad or between foreign countries, in which these persons or firms take part;

2. loans contracted by registered banks and credit institutions; and

3. loans backed by a guarantee from the government.

U.S. Department of Commerce, International Trade Administration

Commercial Banks. After more than a decade of bank restructuring, Cameroon has 10 full-service commercial banks with 60 branches. Eight of Cameroon's 10 commercial banks have correspondence with U.S. banks. Previously, the commercial banks were obliged to hold noninterest-bearing government bonds equivalent to 10 percent of their assets. Commercial banks are no longer required to purchase new government bonds.

Foreign Banks. Foreign direct investments in the banking sector and other financial sectors in Cameroon, including those made by companies in Cameroon that are directly or indirectly under foreign control and those made by branches or subsidiaries of foreign companies in Cameroon, require prior declaration to the Ministry of Economy and Finance. The return of Citibank, a U.S. bank operation, to Cameroon in 1998 has facilitated and improved financial transactions between the United States and Cameroon.

Stock Market

Although Cameroon has no securities or bond market, recent discussions among the six member states of CEMAC indicate a desire to create a regional market.

Insurance Industry

The insurance sector is regulated by Cameroonian laws and monitored by the Ministry of Economy and Finance. The government is fully committed to speeding up the privatization process and to restructuring two public insurance companies still in the government portfolio, the Society of Cameroon Insurance and Reinsurers (SOCAR) and Company of National Reinsurers (CNR).

Other Finance Programs

In Cameroon, the government has a program similar to that of the U.S. Export-Import Bank to finance Cameroonian exports. Transactions are most frequently settled through guaranteed, irrevocable letters of credit.

U.S. Export-Import Bank financing was suspended in 1992, but in 1998, the bank's board of directors voted to resume cooperation with Cameroon for short-term projects from the public sector and medium-term projects from the private sector. Both U.S. exporters and Cameroonian buyers of U.S. goods can apply for bank financing. The U.S. government signed an investment guarantee agreement with Cameroon in 1967. OPIC has been receptive to American firms seeking war, expropriation, and inconvertibility insurance and has guaranteed several ventures in Cameroon. OPIC is currently assessing the country's recent record and appears ready to underwrite viable projects in the future. Cameroon's investment code guarantees protection from noncommercial risk, per the MIGA treaty with Cameroon.

11

Banking Infrastructure

Congo's central bank, the Banque Centrale du Congo, is responsible for supervising the banking system and regulating foreign trade. The central bank was closed to the public in January 1994 due to a shortage of banknotes. In October 1994, the government encouraged its citizens to retain money in the banking sector in order to keep the banking industry from further deterioration. Unfortunately, many banks have since closed their offices as the economic and political situation has declined further.

Persistent high inflation, the collapse of the economy, the insolvency of state-owned financial institutions, and the imprudent use of the central bank to finance deficit spending by the government have over time severely reduced the scope and functions of the banking system. Subsistence activity and the use of informal markets have further reduced the demand for traditional banking services. In addition, highly negative real interest rates have discouraged saving and undermined the banking system's deposit base.

Reform of the Democratic Republic of the Congo's moribund banking system is at the top of the government's economic policy agenda in recognition of the fact that a healthy, well-functioning financial sector is crucial to business activity and revival of the overall economy. The government has already taken steps in this direction by pursuing a balanced budget, avoiding central bank financing of government operations, and raising interest rates toward market levels. It has also moved to strengthen the integrity and supervision of the commercial banks by suspending clearing house privileges for several insolvent (largely state-owned) banks.

Presently, the Democratic Republic of the Congo's banking system is comprised of 12 commercial banks and a development bank, the Société Financière de Développement. Other financial intermediaries include a postal checking system and 19 credit cooperatives.

Citibank Democratic Republic of the Congo, a wholly owned subsidiary of Citicorp, is the only U.S. bank in the country.

The loan portfolios of the banks are at best substandard and largely limited to short-term finance. Prudential supervision of banks is minimal at best, and the legal framework, particularly regarding debt recovery and collateral, is generally unreliable due to the inadequacies of the courts. Most foreign business ventures in the Democratic Republic of the Congo are financed privately, because the country's high-risk atmosphere generally precludes other sources of financing. Exporters usually operate on the basis of irrevocable letters of credit.

The local banking system in the past has been subject to periodic interference from the government, but the current government is committed to market-oriented policies and opposes any kind of intervention in the banking sector.

The Democratic Republic of the Congo's commercial banking system does not engage in project financing, but does provide a limited amount of trade financing. Most commercial banks in the Democratic Republic of the Congo maintain correspondent arrangements with banks operating in the United States. Due to high inflation of the local currency, most large, domestic commercial transactions are carried out in U.S. dollars.

Stock Market

The Democratic Republic of the Congo has no stock market.

Insurance Industry

Information on the Democratic Republic of the Congo's insurance industry is not available.

Other Finance Programs

The U.S. Export-Import Bank is not currently open in the Democratic Republic of the Congo. OPIC offers coverage on a case-by-case basis. The Democratic Republic of the Congo is not a member of MIGA.

13

Banking Infrastructure

The Congolese banking sector is all but moribund. Although some small banks have tried to reopen for business, they are hampered by an unreliable money supply.

The Republic of Congo's banking system is controlled by the BEAC, a multilateral central bank that also serves five other CEMAC countries. The other members are Cameroon, the Central African Republic, Chad, Gabon, and Guinea. BEAC is closely monitored by the French Treasury.

BEAC and the Ministry of Economy, Finance, and Budget regulate exchange transactions, supervise authorized banks and dealers, and regulate open foreign exchange positions.

Long- and short-term bank loans are practically non-existent because there is little official control over prices and wages. Most economic transactions are conducted as barter arrangements, and traditional market pricing mechanisms have ceased to exist, although market prices apply for some goods in rural areas.

Congo's banks are quasi-governmental enterprises in which the state has the majority of shares. The banking industry is open to private investment, but investors must meet criteria set forth by the African Banking Corporation Agreement.

Commercial Banks. In 1992, Congo had five commercial banks. Presently, Congo has three full-service commercial banks and one development bank. The Banque Commerciale Congolaise went out of business in 1992, the Banque Nationale de Développement closed in 1994. The three remaining commercial banks provide services including letters of credit and routine banking services. They are the Union Congolaise de Banques, Banque Internationale du Congo, and Crédit Rural du Congo. Crédit Rural is mostly oriented toward agriculture and industry while the other two banks offer general banking services (exchange transactions and credit). Only the Banque Internationale is open to transactions abroad. All three banks disburse civil servant and military salaries.

Foreign Banks. The Financial Bank, also called Banque Française Intercontinentale, provides financial services to oil companies and other local businesses operating in Congo. A French bank, it is the only foreign-owned bank established in Congo. Other banks do have foreign shareholders.

Stock Market

There is no stock market in the Republic of Congo.

Insurance Industry

The Ministry of Economy, Finance, and Budget and the African Corporation of Insurance Companies regulate the insurance sector. Congo's insurance industry is very limited and is represented by Insurance and Reinsurance of Congo, a member of the Africa Corporation of Insurance Companies (ARC). ARC provides essential insurance coverage, such as automotive, life (about 3 percent of activities), and fire. Automotive insurance, fire insurance, life insurance, and health insurance are not common in Congo but are provided to some extent by the National Social Security Company. Foreign oil companies in Congo also hold insurance coverage from international underwriters. The insurance industry is in the privatization pipeline and will be opened to private investors in the future.

There are no foreign insurance companies offering local services, although some international underwriters may maintain small correspondent offices in Congo.

Other Finance Programs

Congo is a member of MIGA, which offers insurance to new foreign investments against foreign exchange risk, expropriation, and civil unrest. However, MIGA has not resumed coverage for Congo. OPIC, which offered American investors similar insurance protection in the past, has approved no new coverage since 1991, but is looking closely at new applications. OPIC is also accepting applications for investment project financing. U.S. Export-Import Bank financing is open for specially financed transactions.

15

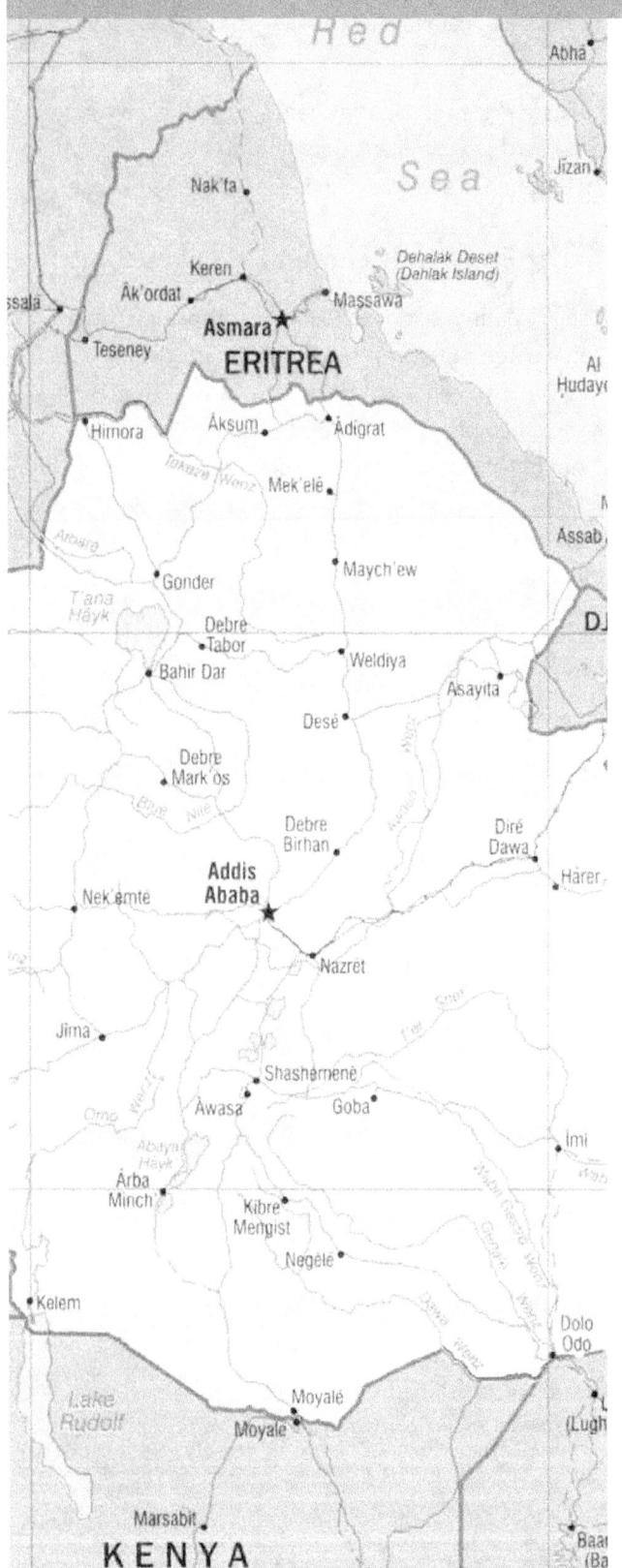

Banking Infrastructure

Efficient banking and other financial services are available in Ethiopia. The National Bank of Ethiopia serves as the central bank and monitors financial sector activities including banking and insurance, as well as activities of the rural credit organizations. Ethiopia does not allow foreign ownership of banks. Local banks maintain a variety of correspondent relationships with foreign banks, including U.S. banks such as Citibank, Bank of America, Bank of New York, and Chase Manhattan Bank. General financing is available to local companies in Ethiopia.

Commercial Banks. Ethiopia has nine commercial banks, of which two are government-owned. Commercial Bank of Ethiopia and the Development Bank of Ethiopia, the government-owned banks, have 164 branches, including one in Djibouti. The seven private commercial banks are: (1) Wegagen Bank, (2) Awash International Bank, (3) Bank of Abyssinia, (4) Dashen Bank, (5) Nile International Bank, (6) United Bank, and (7) Construction and Business Bank.

Commercial Bank of Ethiopia and the first four of the private banks listed above offer savings and checking accounts, extend short-term loans, deal with foreign exchange transactions, provide mail and cable money transfer services, participate in equity investments, provide guarantee services, and perform all other commercial banking activities.

The Development Bank of Ethiopia extends short-, medium-, and long-term loans for viable development projects, including industrial and agricultural projects. It also provides other banking services, such as checking and savings accounts, to its clients. It has 13 main branches and 18 sub-branches in different parts of the country.

Construction and Business Bank provides long-term loans for construction, acquisition, or maintenance of dwellings, community facilities, and real estate develop-

U.S. Department of Commerce, International Trade Administration

ment. In addition, it offers all other commercial banking services to businesses.

Stock Market

A stock market has yet to develop in Ethiopia. Some individuals, private companies, and the Addis Ababa Chamber of Commerce have tried to establish a stock market. The National Bank of Ethiopia has researched the best approach to introduce a stock market.

Insurance Industry

The National Bank of Ethiopia monitors activities of the insurance industry. All classes of insurance services are mainly provided by the Ethiopian Insurance Corporation. Prior to the military regime of 1974–1991, the insurance sector in Ethiopia flourished, with a number of domestic as well as foreign private insurance companies in operation.

When the military regime came to power in 1974, all insurance companies were nationalized, and the Ethiopia Insurance Corporation, a state-owned company, was the only insurer allowed to operate. After the fall of the military regime in 1991, the new government proclaimed market liberalization, which included opening up bank and insurance activity to private participation. Currently, nine insurance companies operate in Ethiopia: Africa Insurance, Awash Insurance, Ethiopian Corporation (which is government owned), Global

Insurance, National Insurance Company of Ethiopia, Nile Insurance Share Company, Nyala Insurance Share Company, United Insurance Share Company, and Universal Insurance Company.

Because foreign ownership is banned, no foreign insurance companies currently operate in Ethiopia.

Other Finance Programs

Ethiopia is currently "off-cover" for the services of U.S. Export-Import Bank programs, except for special finance transactions. Further macroeconomic progress may eventually result in more favorable credit risk ratings, leading to access to bank financing.

A MIGA member, Ethiopia is preparing to sign an agreement with OPIC and has also signed agreements with a number of countries, including Italy, Kuwait, Turkey, and Malaysia. The International Finance Corporation has also begun to provide insurance to the private sector.

17

Banking Infrastructure

Gabon has a well-developed banking system, which includes one development bank and 10 commercial banks. Gabon's banking system is controlled by the BEAC, a multilateral central bank that also serves five other CEMAC countries. The other members are Cameroon, the Central African Republic, Chad, the Republic of Congo, and Guinea. BEAC is closely monitored by the French Treasury.

The central bank interest rate was previously kept very low in order to help moderate the impact on costs and prices, as well as to encourage investments. However, with the higher risks of corporate insolvency in the 1990s, the BEAC tightened credit controls on commercial banks by raising interest rates. The CFA franc, which Gabon uses, is fixed to the French franc. The French government has stated that the same linkage and currency guarantee system will be maintained under the new euro currency arrangement.

The Directorate of Financial Institutions of the Ministry of Finance, Economy, Budget, and Participations supervises borrowing and lending abroad. Exchange control is administered by the ministry, which has partly delegated approval authority to banks for payment and to the BEAC for issues related to the external position of the banks. All exchange transactions relating to foreign countries must be accepted through authorized intermediaries, the Postal Administration, and authorized banks.

Local Banks. Local credit is available to both foreign and local investors on equal terms. The local banking system is relatively sophisticated and offers most corporate banking services or can procure them in Europe. Loans contracted by Gabonese companies with foreign entities are subject to the prior authorization of the Ministry of Finance, Economy, Budget, and Participations. Small and medium-sized enterprises complain that business financing is expensive and difficult to obtain unless the company is established and known to the banking community. Other financing for small and medium-sized firms owned by Gabonese nationals can be obtained from the Development and Expansion Fund, a quasi-governmental organization funded by the African Development Bank and the Banque Gabonaise de Crédit Rural, which offers loans for agricultural enterprises. Local offices of foreign oil companies have used interest rate swaps and euro currency bonds to finance oil field development investments. Exports are usually financed through irrevocable letters of credit. Loans for housing can be obtained from the Crédit Foncier du Gabon.

Commercial Banks. Credit is provided through five main commercial banks: the Banque International de Commerce de l'Industrie du Gabon (a branch of BNP France), Union Gabonaise de Banque (a branch of Crédit Lyonnais), the Banque Gabonaise et Française Internationale (formerly Banque Paribas), Citibank, and the French Intercontinental Bank. The three Gabonese banks are affiliated with French banks and one American bank (Citibank).

Development Bank. The Gabonese Development Bank lends to small and medium-sized companies.

Foreign Banks. Neither the government nor the private sector have made an effort to restrict foreign participation in the banking sector. Foreign companies investing in Gabon must offer shares for purchase by Gabonese nationals for an amount equivalent to at least 10 percent of the company's capital. Financial transfers of less than $8,300 can be freely made to France or within the franc monetary zone by bank means. However, all transfers exceeding this amount require a justification. Private transfers to areas outside of the franc monetary zone are subject to authorizations by the Ministry of Finance.

Foreign-owned banks in Gabon are: Citibank (100 percent); Banque Gabonaise et Française Internationale (43.3 percent owned by Paribas International); Banque Internationale pour Commerce et l'Industrie du Gabon (23.8 percent owned by BNP France); and the Union Gabonaise de Banque (56.25 percent owned by Crédit Lyonnais).

Stock Market

There is no stock market in Gabon, although the country is positioning itself for one in the future.

Insurance Industry

The insurance industry operates and is regulated under the francophone African insurance code and entity Conférence Interafricaine des Marchés d'Assurances (CIMA). The major insurers are AXA Insurances Gabon, Omnium Gabonais d'Assurances et de Reassurances-Groupe Athena/AGF, and Gras Savoye Gabon, all of which have European participation/ownership, and all except the last having a minority stake from the Gabonese government. They offer a range of products. Related companies offer life insurance. Gabon Vie (70 percent foreign interests; 30 percent Gabonese) solely offers life insurance.

Other Finance Programs

OPIC coverage has not been sought for investments in Gabon; however, OPIC has expressed interest in operating in Gabon. Gabon is not a member of MIGA. The U.S. Export-Import Bank is off-cover for Gabon's public credits, but is available for private and specially financed transactions. The government of Gabon has an extended fund facility with the IMF.

19

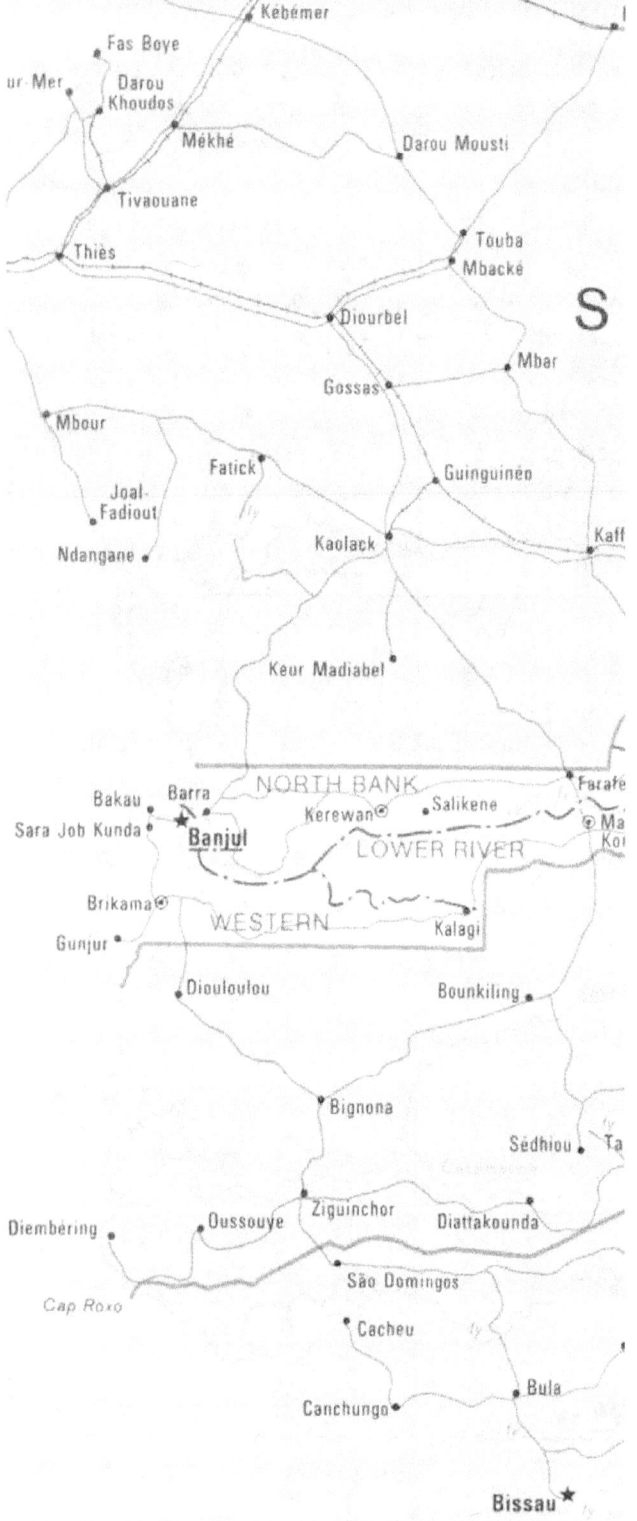

Banking Infrastructure

Banking in Gambia is controlled by the government through the Central Bank of Gambia. The bank issues banking licenses under the Financial Instructions Act of 1974 and monitors, regulates, and supervises the banking system. Besides the central bank, the banking system is built around several financial institutions, mainly six commercial banks, five insurance companies, a number of foreign exchange bureaus and pensions, and provident and housing finance funds. Foreign direct investments in the financial sector are not restricted but must be reported to the central bank for statistical purposes.

Significant government borrowing has created high real interest rates, effectively limiting local capital access to a small and well-established cadre of import-export traders and a few other businesses. Private companies seeking financing not available through local banks are likely to seek offshore financing.

Commercial Banks. There are currently four commercial banks operating in Gambia. The commercial banks offer a wide range of banking and financial services, including trade financing term credit, dealings in foreign exchange and equity participation, acceptance of deposits, short-term credit, loan financing, and savings and current account facilities. The bulk of bank lending is concentrated in the distributive trade sector, due to the low risks and quick returns from this sector. Commercial banks are not allowed to offer deposits in foreign currencies. The government does not provide loans for investors. Foreign investors are expected to bring their own funds.

The commercial banks do not provide long-term financing and their interest rates for short-term financing are usually over 20 percent. However, Gambia does have the Commonwealth Development Corporation, a financial institution that could provide soft long-term loans for agribusinesses.

Stock Market

There is no stock market in Gambia.

Insurance Industry

Gambia has five insurance companies. The insurance companies have not developed sufficient excess resources to make long-term investments. Additional information is not available for Gambia's insurance industry.

Other Finance Programs

Short-term financing from the U.S. Export-Import Bank is available in Gambia to support U.S. exports sales to public-sector buyers. OPIC programs are not presently available in Gambia because of overall restrictions on bilateral assistance to Gambia by the United States. Gambia is a member of MIGA.

Banking Infrastructure

The banking system is supervised and monitored by the central bank, the Bank of Ghana. Ghana's formal banking sector is comprised of seven commercial banks, five merchant banks, three development banks, and more than 100 unit banks. Until recently the sector was dominated by state-owned institutions and showed few signs of competition. Within the past two years, however, the two largest state-owned banks, Ghana Commercial Bank and SSB Bank, Ltd., have been privatized under the government's Divesture Implementation Program, and others are to follow suit in the near future.

Although the government of Ghana encourages foreign investment though the Ghana Investment Promotion Center law, sectors such as banking, non-banking financial institutions, insurance, fishing securities, and real estate are regulated by sector-specific laws that discourage foreign investments.

The formal banking institutions have been unable to provide much genuine intermediation between savers and investors. Demand deposits are the main source of funds for banks, and loans and advances account for a relatively small portion of their assets. High reserve requirements have prevented banks from building up their loan portfolios. Banks have thus tended to prefer the attractive and relatively risk-free returns from holding government securities.

Traditional trade finance instruments such as letters of credit, collections, and funds transfer are available to the exporter.

The nonbank financial institutions, which include the Social Security and National Insurance Trust, the Ghana Stock Exchange, insurance companies, and the discount houses, have yet to emerge as significant players in the financial system. That could change in the medium term with the introduction of new legislation for the sector. The contractual savings institutions, too, have played it safe by investing in short-term government securities. Other than for real estate, these institutions have provided little medium- and long-term finance to the economy.

Commercial Banks. The seven commercial banks (Ghana Commercial Bank, Ltd., Standard Chartered Bank, Ltd, Barclays Bank, Ltd., The Trust Bank, Ltd., Social Security Bank, Ltd., Ghana Co-operative Bank, and International Commercial Bank (Ghana), Ltd.) offer services such as current and savings accounts, telegraphic transfers, safe custody deposits, sale of establishment, and letters of credit. These commercial banks operate 277 branches throughout the country and handle over 70 percent of all banking business. In addition to commercial banking, the Trust Bank and the International Commercial Bank also render merchant banking services.

Merchant Banks. The six merchant banks (Merchant Bank Ghana, Ltd., Ecobank Ghana, Ltd., CAL Merchant Bank, Ltd., First Atlantic Merchant Bank, Ltd., Prudential Bank (Ghana), Ltd., and Metropolitan and Allied Bank, Ltd.) offer services such as acceptances, new issues, private and public offers of shares for sale, underwriting of new issues and offers of shares for sale, corporate finance and consulting services, registrar's services for public and private companies, stockbroking services, management of investment portfolios, and leasing and hire purchase services.

Development Banks. The three development banks provide financial assistance in the following order: The National Investment Bank, an industrial development bank, provides assistance to manufacturing and processing industries including agro-industrial projects. It maintains branches in all regions of the country. The Agricultural Development Bank principally serves the agricultural sector and has 31 branches throughout Ghana. The Bank for Housing and Construction finances the construction and housing sectors and has 12 branches in Ghana. These development banks also provide commercial banking services.

Rural Banks. Rural banks are unit banks established to provide facilities for the rural communities in which they are located. They are owned, managed, and patronized by local residents. Some of these banks also operate agencies that cater to communities located far from the bank's facilities. Savings mobilized through rural banks are invested in small-scale agricultural activities, cottage industries, transportation, and trading. There are currently 123 rural banks in the country.

Ghanian banks have correspondent arrangements with the following U.S. banks: Barclays Bank, Citibank, Bankers Trust, Standard Chartered Bank of America, Morgan Guaranty Trust, Chemical Bank, ABN-AMRO Bank, and First Union National Bank.

Stock Market

The Ghana Stock Exchange (GSE) is a nongovernmental private-sector initiative, that was incorporated in July 1989 with trading commencing in 1990. GSE's regulations are designed to protect investors. The GSE council has a supervisory role in order to prevent fraud and malpractice, with the power to suspend or expel any member who contravenes any of the regulations of the exchange. Currently, the exchange has 12 licensed dealing members and 22 listed companies. There are two corporate bonds currently listed. Most of the industries are subsidiaries of multinational companies such as Unilever, Standard Chartered, and Guinness.

Capital gains on securities listed on the GSE were exempted from tax until November 12, 2000; however, there is a 10 percent withholding tax on dividend income for all investors, both local and foreign. The original capital invested, capital gains, dividends, or interest earned and related earnings and refunds are fully and freely remittable.

Ghanaians externally resident and foreigners resident in Ghana may purchase securities listed on the GSE without any restrictions. Nonresident Ghanaians and foreigners require permission for securities that are not listed on the GSE. Individual holdings and total holdings of all nonresidents in any one security listed on the GSE may not exceed 10 percent and 74 percent respectively. For companies not listed on the GSE, nonresident participation requires the following minimum equity injections to acquire shares: (1) $10,000 or its equivalent in capital goods when the enterprise is a joint venture; (2) $50,000 or its equivalent in capital goods when the enterprise is wholly owned by a non-

Ghanaian; and (3) $300,000 or its equivalent in capital goods in the case of a trading enterprise involved only in the purchasing and selling of goods that is either wholly or partly owned by a non-Ghanaian and that employs at least 10 Ghanaians.

Insurance Industry

Insurance in Ghana dates back to the late 19th and early 20th centuries, when it was introduced to West Africa by British trading and commercial interests. It is still predominately a nonlife industry writing traditional lines such as motor, fire, marine, and general accident. The insurance industry is regulated by the National Insurance Commission, an independent regulator established under Ghana's 1989 insurance law. The commission has its own board of directors, with the commissioner of insurance as its chief executive.

Life and health insurance policies are written in Ghana, but long-term insurance still comprises only about 10 percent of the market. Almost any kind of insurance policy is available through local companies and their overseas reinsurers. Ghana is a very small market, with a total gross premium income of only about $40 million. The industry is, however, changing very fast, and premium income has doubled during the last four years. Life insurance and pensions are expected to grow very quickly. There are 21 registered insurance and reinsurance companies. The top four biggest companies dominate the market with 90 percent of the market.

Foreigners may participate as shareholders of an insurance company provided that at least 40 percent of the equity is held by Ghanaians. There are no foreign insurance companies established in Ghana, although foreign individuals and institutions hold equity shares in Ghanaian insurance companies. The German insurer, Munich Re Group, has a liaison office in the country.

Other Finance Programs

For private-sector projects, the International Finance Corporation and OPIC offer investment insurance and loan programs in Ghana.

OPIC launched the Modern Africa Growth Fund and the Africa Infrastructure Investment Fund, which are sources of information on investment in Ghana.

Substantial potential exists for increased OPIC activity on behalf of firms planning new investment, particularly in the mining, agro-processing, and manufacturing sectors.

The African Project Development Facility and the International Finance Corporation's African Investment Program are other sources of information.

Ghana is a member of MIGA, which provides insurance to foreign investors against non-commercial risks.

The U.S. Trade and Development Agency offers funds to finance feasibility studies and loans to finance Ghanian government-sponsored procurement.

The U.S. Export-Import Bank offers foreign buyers medium- and long-term loans for up to 85 percent of the contract price at fixed interest rates for the purchase of U.S. capital equipment and services that face officially subsidized foreign competition.

U.S. Department of Commerce, International Trade Administration

GUINEA

Guinea

....	International boundary
-----------	Region boundary
★	National capital
◉	Region capital
....	Railroad
....	Road

Regions have the same names as their capitals

Banking Infrastructure

The Central Bank of the Republic of Guinea has the authority to control the banking sector. Guinea's banking system is controlled by the BEAC, a multilateral central bank that also serves five other CEMAC countries. The other members are Cameroon, the Central African Republic, Chad, the Republic of Congo, and Gabon. BEAC is closely monitored by the French Treasury.

The Guinean banking system is composed of six active banks, including Banque Islamique de Guinée, Banque Internationale pour le Commerce et l'Industrie de Guinée, Société Générale des Banques en Guinée, Union Internationale des Banques en Guinée, Banque Populaire Maroco-Guinéenne, and International Commercial Bank. The banking sector is largely controlled by foreign-owned banks, which include four French banks, a Moroccan bank, and an Islamic bank.

Guinea's banks prefer to finance trade. Guinea's banking structure lacks a well-trained cadre of managerial and technical personnel. The banking sector has a narrow base, is very fragile, and is unable to meet the development needs of the private sector. Since banks are conservative and risk-averse, there is not a significant amount of capital available to finance large investments. Guinea's banking sector experienced heightened instability in 1997, resulting in the closure of one bank and a pledge to restructure three other banks, with help from the IMF and the World Bank. The government of Guinea has committed itself to economic and judicial reform in order to attract foreign investments and develop the private sector.

Commercial Banks. Guinea's commercial banking sector was the subject of legal reforms in 1985 and 1986. Currently, the commercial bank structure is being restructured with help from the IMF and the World Bank. Commercial banks favor short-term lending at high interest rates (25 to 30 percent). The commercial banks generally limit their activities to short- and medium term-finance, with very limited lending practices. Private companies seeking financing not available through local banks are likely to seek offshore financing. Several donor programs have set up credit guarantee mechanisms through the commercial banks for agricultural and small enterprise lending. These, however, are difficult for expatriates to access. Most U.S. exporters dealing with Guinean importers receive direct payment through international transfer. If not, exporters are encouraged to insist upon an irrevocable letter of credit before shipping products to Guinea.

Local Banks. The domestic banking sector does lend to local companies. Of all loans granted in 1986, 29.6 percent were given to private-sector companies. By 1998, this number had climbed to 88.4 percent. Most are short-term loans to small private merchants. In 1998, mid- and long-term loans represented only 15.2 percent of the total loans given to the private sector. Of the total private-sector loans, 55 percent went to merchants.

Local banks with correspondent U.S. banking arrangements include Banque Internationale de Commerce et Industrie, the French American Banking Corporation, Banque National de Paris New York branch, Société Generale de Banques en Guinée, Banque Islamique de Guinée, and Union Internationale de Banque en Guinée.

Stock Market

There is no stock market established in Guinea.

Insurance Industry

Insurance information is not available.

Other Finance Programs

Guinea is eligible only for short-term private U.S. Export-Import Bank programs. The U.S. Department of Agriculture export promotion programs offer a dairy export incentive program (the West Africa Regional GSM-102 Export Credit Guarantee program) and a wheat export enhancement program.

The IMF and the World Bank provide limited and expensive services, with restricted financing options.

The African Development Bank's private-sector program has some funding available for development-oriented business projects. OPIC will accept applications for investment projects in Guinea. The U.S. Trade and Development Agency has a small program to assist in the financing of feasibility studies that meet significant U.S. export criteria. In 1989, Guinea signed the convention for MIGA. It was ratified in 1993.

U.S. Department of Commerce, International Trade Administration

THE GAMBIA

Konka

Kalaji

Bounkiling

SEN

Kol

Bignona

Sédhiou

Banbali

Tanaf

Ziguinchor

Diattakounda

Farim

Sao Domingos

Ignore

Barro

Cacheu

Bissorã

Bula

Canchungo

Mansôa

Safim

Nhacra

Cumeré

Quinhámel

★ Bissau

Enxudé

Ondame

Fulacunda

QUINAR.

Ilha de Bolama

Bolama

Ilha Formosa

ÓS   BOLAMA

Bubaque

Catió

a de ngo

Ilha Roxa

Cacine

nea-Bissau

l boundary	⊛	Region capital
ndary	┼┼┼┼ Railroad	
pital	──── Road	

40 Kilometers

40 Miles

Banking Infrastructure

Guinea-Bissau's banking system is governed by the BCEAO. Guinea-Bissau, along with seven other franc zone nations, is a member of the WAEMU. Other member countries are Benin, Burkina Faso, Ivory Coast, Mali, Niger, Senegal, and Togo.

WAEMU established the BCEAO, which issued the CFA franc, the unit of currency for the member states, and established policies governing interest rates. BCEAO banking supervision, strengthened by the role of the WAEMU Banking Commission, has enhanced the enforcement and regulatory provisions of the banking system. BCEAO also has the power to monitor other financial institutions.

Exchange control is administered by the director of the treasury in the Ministry of Economy and Finance. All foreign direct investments are subject to prior declaration to the ministry. In 1962, the WAEMU signed an agreement that guaranteed the convertibility of the CFA and French francs, and established operations accounts for each country with the French treasury in order to centralize their reserves. The signatories also agreed to the free circulation of capital within the union. Since 1962, the WAEMU has modified its system gradually to grant greater monetary autonomy to the African member states.

Lending to nonresidents must be approved by the ministry. There are no restrictions if their operations involve commercial credits. Prior authorization from the ministry is required for loans, financial credits, or the purchase of securities abroad.

Stock Market

Guinea-Bissau is a member of the Bourse Régionale des Valeurs Mobilières, a regional stock market located in Abidjan, Ivory Coast. Established in 1996, this regional stock market became effective in the last three months of 1998. This exchange links Guinea-Bissau with the other French-speaking member countries of the West African Economic and Monetary Union: Benin, Burkina Faso, Ivory Coast, Mali, Niger, Senegal, and Togo.

The issuance and sale of securities in Guinea-Bissau by nonresidents require prior authorization from the Ministry of Economy and Finance. After obtaining prior authorization from the ministry, a resident may purchase securities issued or sold by a nonresident who has also received prior authorization. There is no restriction on the sale of securities constituting the liquidation of an investment when it takes the form of a transfer between a nonresident and a resident, provided that the financial settlement of the operation is in order. The settlement of a securities operation by outward transfer or by deposit to a nonresident's account requires an exchange authorization that must be approved by the ministry. It also requires documents attesting to the validity of the operation.

Residents are free to sell the shares of resident companies abroad. If the effect of such operations is to place resident Guinea-Bissau companies under foreign control, the foreign investors must make a prior decla-

ration to the ministry. The sale of securities constituting the liquidation of an investment abroad is subject to prior declaration to the ministry, and if the proceeds are foreign exchange from the sale of liquidation, they must be surrendered and sold to an authorized intermediary bank.

Insurance Industry

Insurance industry information is not available.

Other Finance Programs

Guinea-Bissau is eligible only for short-term U.S. Export-Import Bank financed transactions. OPIC will accept applications for investment projects in Guinea-Bissau. Guinea-Bissau is not a member of MIGA.

28

Banking Infrastructure

The Ivory Coast's banking system is governed by the BCEAO. The Ivory Coast, along with seven other franc zone nations, is a member of the WAEMU. Other member countries are Benin, Burkina Faso, Guinea-Bissau, Mali, Niger, Senegal, and Togo.

WAEMU established the BCEAO, which issued the CFA franc, the unit of currency for the member states, and established policies governing interest rates. BCEAO banking supervision, strengthened by the role of the WAEMU Banking Commission, has enhanced the enforcement and regulatory provisions of the banking system. BCEAO also has the power to monitor other financial institutions.

Banking supervision, strengthened by the role of the WAEMU Banking Commission, will also be pursued through the strict enforcement of regulatory and prudential provision in order to enhance the credibility of the banking system.

Exchange control is administered by the director of the treasury in the ministry of Economy and Finance. In 1962, the WAEMU signed an agreement that guaranteed the convertibility of the CFA and French francs, and established operations accounts for each country with the French treasury in order to centralize their reserves. The signatories also agreed to the free circulation of capital within the union. Since 1962, the WAEMU has modified its system gradually to grant greater monetary autonomy to the African member states.

Foreign investments in the financial sectors are subject to prior declaration to the ministry, which has a period of two months in which to request the suspension of the operation. The transfer of a direct investment by a nonresident to another nonresident is also subject to prior declaration. Special incentives are provided for foreign and domestic investments in certain priority sectors and geographical areas.

Ivory Coast has 17 credit and loan banks (11 com-

29

mercial banks and six specialized credit banks), nine foreign bank offices with limited activity, 16 registered credit or leasing institutions, and seven organizations similar to credit unions. More than half of bank ownership remains in foreign control: six of the 11 commercial banks are branches of foreign banks (including three American institutions). Of the 11 banks, Ivorians own no more than 48.4 percent. Three French bank subsidiaries and the subsidiary of a Belgian bank dominate the market. Citibank, which mainly serves large multinational companies, is present in Abidjan. Ecobank is regarded as a progressive and reliable regional bank. HSBC Equator Bank has nonretail operations in Abidjan, Standard Chartered (U.K.) plans to open a retail bank by early 2001.

Ivorian Banks and their correspondent U.S. banks are Société Générale de Banques en Côte d'Ivoire, Crédit Commercial de France, Banque Nationale de Paris, Crédit Lyonnais, Citibank, Banque Atlantique, Paribas, Ecobank, Banque de l'Habitat de Côte d'Ivoire (specializes in housing), and Barclays Bank (purchased in April 1995 by Financial Bank, a Franco-Swiss financial consortium with operations in Benin, Senegal, and Togo).

Commercial Banks. Commercial lenders tend to rely more on collateral than on the prospective incomes and cash flows of borrowers. Financing is generally available for short-term (one year or less), private-sector projects. Prior to devaluation of the CFA franc, lending was highly restricted and loan rates high (at 18 percent); in an effort to control the inflationary impact of devaluation, rates rose even higher. Since the devaluation, flight capital has returned and liquidity within the system has increased substantially. Few loans, however, have been made due to limited opportunities, high interest rates, repayment concerns, and apprehension that the Ivorian government has yet to address the huge public debt. Improvement in the fiscal position should enable the government to reduce its indebtedness to the banking system, so as to make more room for increased bank lending to the private sector. The current lending rate ranges from 10 to 17 percent. Consequently, it is the general rule that medium- to long-term public sector projects are financed by multilateral lending institutions such as the World Bank or the African Development Bank or by European foreign aid programs.

Stock Market

The Abidjan Stock Exchange was established in 1974 and started trading in 1976 to encourage domestic investment and to provide Ivorian industries with access to the international financial market. The exchange closed at the end of December 1997. In September 1998, the world's first regional stock exchange, the Bourse Régionale des Valeurs Mobilières (BRVM) was established. The new exchange links Ivory Coast with the other French-speaking member countries of the West African Economic and Monetary Union: Benin, Burkina Faso, Guinea-Bissau, Mali, Niger, Senegal, and Togo. Of an estimated 700 companies in the Ivory Coast, the shares of only 30 were quoted on the BRVM exchange.

There are no restrictions on foreign ownership, although the authorities reserve the right to set foreign ownership limits. Most investors in the quoted companies were foreign residents or businesses; Ivorians owned only 30 percent of the shares.

Insurance Industry

Ivory Coast has a high number of insurance companies (30 firms), but average insurance premiums are low (0.05 percent of GDP). All of these insurance companies are privately owned. The companies operate under an insurance law but are not regulated by the government. They are affiliated with the African Council of Insurance Companies, and offer short-term and long-term insurance. Weak government supervision and fragmented markets have allowed the proliferation of financially nonviable insurance companies.

The insurance industry is subject to licensing requirements, but there are no restrictions aimed at limiting foreign ownership.

Other Finance Programs

The International Finance Corporation and the OPIC provide programs that include loans, loan guarantees, and insurance products. The U.S. Export-Import Bank offers short-term financing for U.S. export sales to public sector buyers in Ivory Coast. The U.S. Trade and Development Agency, the World Bank, and the African

Development Bank offer funds to finance feasibility studies and loans to finance Ivorian government-sponsored procurement. Ivory Coast is a member of MIGA.

ETHIOPIA

Moyale

EASTERN

Marsabit

RIFT

VALLEY

Mad Gast

Isiolo

Nyahururu Falls

Nanyuki

Nakuru

Nyeri

Embu

Kindaruma dams

CENTRAL

Thika

arok

EASTERN

Nairobi

NAIROBI AREA

C

Magadi

y

Arusha

Moshi

Voi

Nyumba ya Mungu dam

TANZANIA

U.S. Department of Commerce, International Trade Administration

Banking Infrastructure

Kenya has a well-developed banking industry that is regulated by the Central Bank of Kenya. The banking system has weathered several crises, the most recent in 1993 when monthly inflation reached 100 percent. Conversion in 1994–1996 of most of Kenya's finance companies into banks has gone surprisingly smoothly.

At the time of its independence in 1963, Kenya inherited a financial system typical of all British colonies in Africa. The financial system consisted of a central bank, a commercial banking system, a Post Office Savings Bank, and a small number of nonbank financial institutions. The nonbank financial sector has since grown into a substantial, sophisticated one providing mortgage finance, insurance, and other nonbank financial services. The banking sector is comprised of 50 domestic and foreign commercial banks with branches, agencies, and other outlets throughout the country; 19 nonbank financial institutions with an excellent branch network in Kenya's major cities; 6 building societies; 37 insurance companies; 7 development finance companies providing long-term finance; the Post Office Savings Bank, with a large network of branches around the country; and over 1,500 loosely structured savings and credit unions.

In spite of the number of established banks, the banking sector is essentially dominated by four major commercial banks — Kenya Commercial Bank, National Bank of Kenya, Barclays Bank Kenya, and Standard Chartered — with an established tradition of working together. The Kenyan government does not have a specialized financial institution exclusively focusing on export/import business like an export/import bank. Most projects in Kenya are financed through bilateral agreements.

With the marked growth of the Kenyan economy over the last several years, financial houses have played an important role in attracting local and foreign investment into the liberalized market. There are many important financial institutions in the country that offer quality services to their clients. Citibank and First American Bank are the two known U.S.-owned banks operating in Kenya.

Stock Market

The stock market in Kenya is monitored and supervised by the Capital Markets Authority, which was established in 1990. The Nairobi Stock Exchange, founded in 1954, is the only licensed trading exchange in the country. It originally started as a private association, but is now a fully fledged stock market. Kenya has a small capital market, consisting of the government-controlled Capital Markets Authority, one securities exchange, 20 brokers, several dealers, and numerous financial advisors. Operating on an open-try system, the exchange trades in stocks from 62 publicly quoted companies.

The opening of the Nairobi stock exchange to foreign investors in January 1995 marked the first time that foreigners had been allowed to invest in local companies in Kenya but there are restrictions. Foreign ownership of firms listed on the exchange cannot exceed 40 percent, with a 5 percent limit on individual foreign investment.

With the expansion of the Kenyan economy over the last several years, the Nairobi Stock Exchange has played an important role in attracting local and foreign investment into the liberalized market. There are many important stock brokerage firms in the country that offer quality services to their clients.

Insurance Industry

The insurance industry in Kenya was established more than 70 years ago. The commissioner of insurance monitors the industry. In order to invest in the insurance industry, a company must be incorporated and is required to have at least 33 percent local ownership. In Kenya, many insurance firms offer a wide range of policies ranging from vehicle, life, mortgage, home, and medical insurance. Perhaps two of the best insurance companies in Kenya are Mercantile Life and the General Assurance Company, Ltd. One U.S. insurance company active in the Kenyan market is American Life Insurance, which is partially owned by a Kenyan company.

There are no export insurance programs available at present, but Kenya's Seventh National Development Plan states that the government is considering the creation of an export credit and guarantee scheme to be run by a trade bank.

Other Finance Programs

Kenya is currently open for short-term, medium-term, and specially financed transactions from the U.S. Export-Import Bank. Even though Kenya is off-cover for other bank programs, a special Export-Import Bank program for Africa has been initiated whereby short-term bank programs may be made available in the private sector for importers with established credit ratings/experience with a reputable international bank.

OPIC programs are generally available in Kenya. The approval procedures vary on a case-by-case basis. Kenya is a member of MIGA.

33

Banking Infrastructure

Malawi has a sound banking sector, regulated and supervised by its central bank, the Reserve Bank of Malawi. There are five full-service commercial banks: the National Bank of Malawi; Indefinance; Commercial Bank of Malawi (established in 1995); the First Merchant Bank, Ltd.; and the Finance Bank of Malawi.

The Malawi government owns (through direct and indirect shareholdings) both the National Bank and the Commercial Bank, the country's two largest commercial banks. Both banks operate on a commercial, for-profit basis.

Malawi banks have correspondent arrangements with the following U.S. banks: Citibank, Chemical Bank, Bank of New York, Bank of America, Equator Bank, Barclays Bank, Standard Chartered, and Chase Manhattan.

Malawi kwacha-denominated financing is available from Malawi's commercial institutions. Credit is allocated on market terms, and foreign investors are eligible to apply for it.

Imports into Malawi are financed primarily through secured letters of credit.

In Malawi, other financial institutions also provide financing. They are the Investment and Development Bank of Malawi, Investment and Development Fund of Malawi, Finance Corporation of Malawi, Leasing and Finance Company of Malawi, Malawi Savings Bank, the New Building Society, the Malawi Rural Finance Company, and the Malawi Development Corporation.

Stock Market

The Malawi Stock Exchange is governed by the Capital Markets Development Act of 1990 and the Capital Market Development Regulations Act of 1992. The exchange is supervised by a committee composed of representatives from the central bank, the government, and the private sector. Stockbrokers Malawi, Ltd., is the only registered stockbroker in Malawi. It has run a secondary market in government securities since March 1995. Both local and foreign investors have equal access to purchasing securities. Stockbrokers Malawi, Ltd., also began trading shares of companies toward the end of 1996 following the listing of shares of the National Insurance Company of Malawi. Through the Southern Africa Development Community stock exchanges cooperation initiative, Malawi and other community markets are taking steps to harmonize listing requirements.

Foreign investment is allowed, but limited to five percent of issued share capital for one foreign investor and 49 percent of issued share capital in total.

Insurance Industry

There is no information available covering the Malawi insurance industry.

Other Finance Programs

OPIC has had an investment guarantee agreement with Malawi since 1967. U.S. Export-Import Bank financing is only available for public and private short-term and specially financed transactions. The World Bank, through its International Development Agency, is Malawi's most consistent international source of financing for public projects. The African Development Bank and its affiliated fund are another major source of project financing. The U.S. Agency for International Development, the World Bank, and the African Development Bank/Fund are the major donors for projects in which U.S. firms are eligible to participate. Malawi is also a member of MIGA.

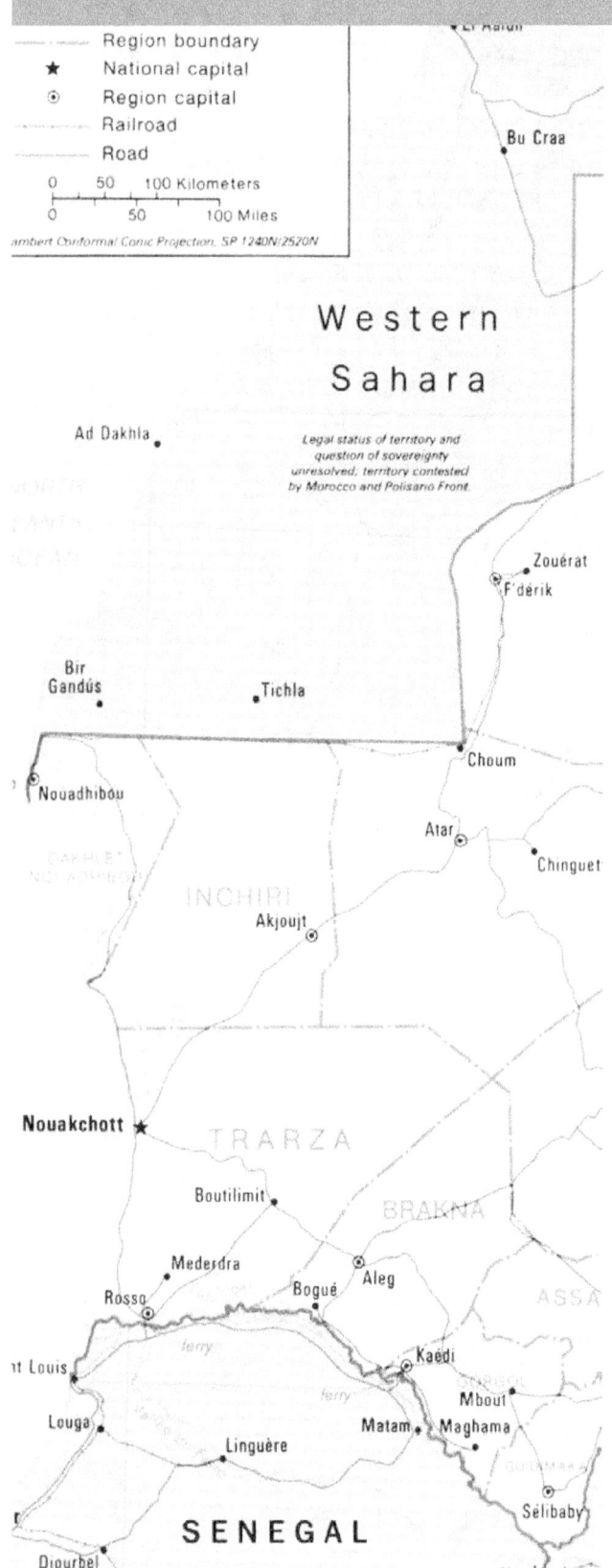

Region boundary
★ National capital
⊙ Region capital
Railroad
Road

0   50   100 Kilometers

0   50   100 Miles

Lambert Conformal Conic Projection, SP 1240N/2520N

Banking Infrastructure

The Central Bank of Mauritania has the authority to supervise and enforce banking standards through the examination of banks' financial reports. The government of Mauritania has privatized all commercial banks, liquidated the development bank, encouraged the creation of savings banks, and promoted the creation of rural cooperatives. Promoting the creation of rural cooperatives has increased capital and brought stricter management. As a result, the national deposit has been adequately funded and loans continue to be contracted, but with more caution.

In spite of the government's efforts to improve the banking sector, commercial banks continue to play a limited role in financing the national economy. High interest rates (23 to 27 percent) discourage most investors from using bank loans, and some business owners feel that the regulatory system is still inadequate. Private citizens are often reluctant to put their money into banks because experience (especially pre-reform) has taught them that deposits are not always available on demand. In addition, privatization has tended to increase socioeconomic inequities, since the local business groups that own the banks make sure that their shareholders and associates receive priority for obtaining scarce foreign currency. However, liberalization of the exchange system and the authorization to create private exchange offices have attenuated these historic tendencies.

Banking sector reform has been a critical goal of the government's economic reorganization. The accounting system and regulations covering investments are modeled on French conventions. After the banking sector was restructured and a computerized system was introduced, banking management improved, but deficiencies persist in the enforcement of laws and regulations.

Mauritanian government policies do not discourage the free flow of financial resources. Credit is allocated on market terms. There are no restrictions on access to local financial institutions by foreign investors, although most prefer external financing. The government's economic programs have put into place selective credit policies that give priority to productive sectors of the economy.

Commercial Banks. Of the seven commercial banks in Mauritania, five are completely private. The two banks that still have government ownership are the Chinguitty Bank, which is 50 percent owned by the Mauritania government and 50 percent by the Libyan government, and the Banque Albaraka Mauritanienne Islamique, which is 10 percent government-owned and 90 percent privately held.

In conjunction with privatization, the government of Mauritania introduced a new banking law to reinforce banking supervision of the commercial banks in order to have a system that guarantees and protects deposits made by private individuals. To enforce the law, the central bank exercises supervision over the commercial banks. The banks are supervised on a consolidated basis founded on an examination of a set of ratios known as "ratios de prudence." The commercial banks are required to send their financial statement to the central bank monthly. Each bank has an office for internal control, which knows activities and prepares financial reports and statements for the central bank and its own top management. However, if necessary, the central bank can delegate inspectors to verify the methods of calculation used by the banks to prepare their financial statements or determine their ratios. Moreover, each bank must be examined annually by an external auditor approved by the Office of Audit. This external examination is required by the central bank under the instructions of the World Bank and the IMF.

All commercial banks must respect the regulations presented in the banking law and are required to comply with international accounting standards. Presently, they are using a new accounting plan, based on the French-speaking countries' accounting system. From 1994, all bank financial reports have to be prepared according to the norms and regulations of the new accounting plan.

Local Banks. Domestic banks lend to local companies, mostly trade companies for short- and medium- terms only. Guarantees required by commercial banks, even for borrowers with established credit, are high compared to the principal amounts. So while general financing is available to local businesspeople, the terms often make it unattractive.

Stock Market

Mauritania does not have a stock market.

Insurance Industry

Mauritania has two insurance companies, but information on them is not available.

Other Finance Programs

Mauritania is currently eligible for the U.S. Export-Import Bank's short-term financing, as well as OPIC financing and insurance programs. The Foreign Credit Insurance Association insures certain purchases of American products by the state mining company. Mauritania is a member of MIGA.

37

Banking Infrastructure

The banking system in Mozambique is small but diversifying. The country privatized its banking system in the early 1990s, soon after abandoning socialism. The central bank, the Banco de Moçambique, regulates and administers control over the banking system. Recent reforms have included the liberalization of foreign exchange markets, the privatization of the largest state commercial bank, the institution of indirect monetary control by the central bank, the overall liberalization of financial markets, and preparations for the opening of a small stock exchange in Maputo.

The financial system consists of one central bank, 10 commercial banks (all privately owned), and one investment bank with private capital, four credit cooperatives, one leasing company, and 27 exchange bureaus.

The Mozambican banking sector is dominated by the Portuguese firm Banco Commercial Portugues, which owns the country's two largest commercial banks and has 70 percent of the market.

Commercial Banks. The Banco Commercial de Moçambique dominates commercial banking, although market shares have adjusted to accommodate new entrants. It is the only bank with branches nationwide, but has experienced unexplained losses of $120 million in 1999, raising doubts about its continued commercial viability. The government sold 51 percent of the bank to a consortium led by Banco Portugues Mello, which was itself later bought by Banco Commercial Portugues. The government continues to hold 49 percent of the bank's shares, meaning it will be responsible for 49 percent of the loan now necessary to keep it solvent.

In 1999, the Banco Internacional de Moçambique acquired the local operations of Banco Portugues do Atlantico, due to a parent company merger in Portugal. With the sale of Banco Commercial de Moçambique and the entry of Banco International de Moçambique, the banking services market seems to have received an

U.S. Department of Commerce, International Trade Administration

injection of much-needed competition. Banco International is the sector's innovation leader, with specialized corporate express and private banking divisions. The January 2000 acquisition of Grupo Mello by Banco Commercial Portugues has not yet resulted in a merger of the two banks. In fact, Banco Commercial Portugues claims that it intends to maintain the banks as separate entities, although there is no anti-trust legislation to prevent their merger. Both banks are now led by the same chairman, Mario Machungo, the former, prime minister of Mozambique. The two banks have, however, joined forces to create Novobank, the most recent bank to open in Mozambique. It will operate as a micro-credit lending window for the existing banks.

Several other private commercial banks operate in Mozambique:

• Banco Standard Totta (40 percent owned by Standard Bank of South Africa and 55 percent by Banco Totta & Açores of Portugal) has been rebuilding its pre-war bank network. It has expanded beyond the fee-for-service and letter of credit business for which it was known during Mozambique's leaner years.

• Banco de Fomento e Exterior, which is based in Portugal.

• Banco Austral, which resulted from the government's sale of Banco Popular de Desenvolvimento (Mozambique's second largest bank) to a consortium led by Southern Berhad Bank of Malaysia in 1997. Banco Popular subsequently changed its name to Banco Austral. Banco Austral promptly lowered its lending rates and has continued to lead the way for consumer loans in this regard.

• Banco Commercial e de Investimento entered the market in 1997 and expanded into commercial banking after Caixa Geral of Portugal assumed control.

• Equator Bank, based in Hartford, Connecticut, but now owned by the Hong Kong and Shanghai Bank. It maintains an office in Maputo that focuses primarily on trade finance.

• Unio Commercial de Bancos, backed by Mauritian interests, opened a Maputo branch in late 1999.

• Nedbank, an important bank in South Africa, recently opened an office in Maputo in conjunction with BNP Paribas of France.

Local Banks. The local banking system best serves established companies with well-known track records. Financing for entrepreneurs is problematic. Interest rates for small or new companies approach 20 percent, although rates may be more favorable for known clients. Availability of credit in rural areas and small towns is very limited.

American Banks. No American commercial banks operate in Mozambique, but three have regional offices. Citibank has traditionally conducted most of its business with Mozambique from its regional office in Nairobi, but is now transferring these operations to its Johannesburg office. Chase Manhattan/Chemical Bank and J.P. Morgan also handle their Mozambican operations from their offices in South Africa. Citibank, the Bank of New York, Chase Manhattan, Corestates (now part of First Union), and the Bank of America all have correspondent relationships with local banks.

Stock Market

The stock market is a recent development in Mozambique. The government created a small stock exchange, the Bolsa de Valores de Moçambique, in October 1999 when it sold the government's 20 percent share in Cervejas de Mozambique. (The remaining 80 percent of the privatized brewery belongs to a South African company that won a privatization bid in the mid-1990s.) Fourteen other companies are in the process of being admitted to the stock market. (According to the stock market's rules, companies need to have at least $1.5 million for them to be admitted.) The exchange is also involved in selling treasury bills valued at $5 million.

Insurance Industry

Mozambique's Ministry of Planning and Finance sponsors insurance activities. There are six insurance companies in Mozambique. As of the third quarter of 1999, the government approved the creation of the Inspeccão General de Seguros, which is responsible for the supervision of the insurance industry. (An entity with the same designation existed in the colonial era, but it ceased operations soon after independence, and its functions were taken over by the Public Insurance Company, which now operates as another insurance company).

Other Finance Programs

OPIC provides coverage to U.S. investments in Mozambique. In late 1994, Mozambique joined MIGA. The U.S. Export-Import Bank now covers Mozambique. The International Finance Corporation and the Commonwealth Development Corporation provide medium-term loans and equity finance.

40

NAMIBIA

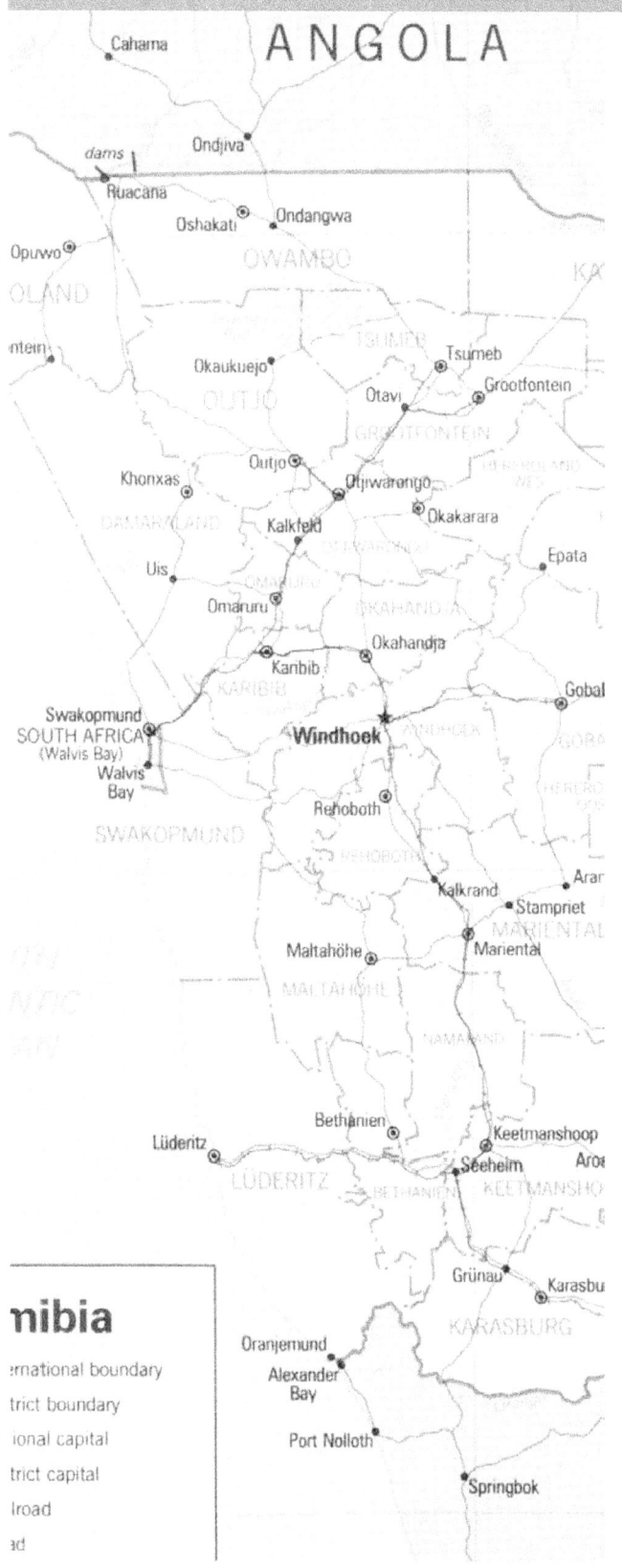

ANGOLA

Cahama
Ondjiva
dams
Ruacana
Oshakati · Ondangwa
Opuwo
OWAMBO
Okaukuejo
Tsumeb
Otavi · Grootfontein
Outjo
Khonxas
Otjiwarongo
Kalkfeld
Okakarara
Uis
Epata
Omaruru
Okahandja
Kanbib
Gobal
Swakopmund
SOUTH AFRICA
(Walvis Bay)
Walvis
Bay
Windhoek
Rehoboth
Arar
Kalkrand · Stampriet
Maltahöhe
Mariental
Bethanien
Lüderitz
Keetmanshoop
Seeheim
Aro
Grünau · Karasbu

nibia

ernational boundary
trict boundary
ional capital
trict capital
lroad
ad

Oranjemund
Alexander
Bay
Port Nolloth
Springbok

Banking Infrastructure

The Central Bank of Namibia regulates its banks through the Banking Institutions Act of 1998, and has progressively taken over functions previously performed by the South African Reserve Bank. With the launch of Namibia's own currency in September 1993, the bank became a fully operative central bank. The policy of the Bank of Namibia regarding banking institutions is to enforce prudent banking standards and practices based on internationally accepted standards, such as the basic core principles for effective banking supervision. The banking system is modern and efficient. Namibian banks are capable of handling international financial transactions and trade finance.

There are nine public finance institutions, including the Development Fund of Namibia and the Agricultural Bank of Namibia. All banks provide comprehensive domestic and international services. Short-term insurance and life insurance brokerage, estate planning, and factoring are some of the ancillary services provided by the banking sector.

The central bank, the Ministry of Finance, and the financial sectors are actively pursuing the establishment of financial institutions and markets, such as quasi-governmental bills, debentures, and bonds, government Treasury bills, and negotiable certificates of deposit.

A domestic money market and foreign exchange market are rapidly developing. Local interbank lending is limited due to the size of the market, and local banks are often referred to the South African interbank market.

Commercial Banks. There are six commercial banks, the largest being First National Bank of Namibia, Ltd., Standard Bank Namibia, Ltd., and the Commercial Bank of Namibia, Ltd. The commercial banks in Namibia provide comprehensive domestic and international banking services. Project financing is available for agricultural products, commercial fishing, tourism, housing, and minerals and mining.

41

Foreign Banks. There are no restrictions on foreign investments in the banking industry. The foreign-owned banks are Standard Bank Namibia, Ltd., which is 100 percent owned by Standard Bank Investment Corporation, Ltd., of South Africa; First National Bank of Namibia, Ltd., which is 78 percent owned by First National Bank Holdings, Ltd., of South Africa and 22 percent locally owned; Commercial Bank of Namibia, Ltd., 92.66 percent of which is owned by the Namibian Banking Corporation, Ltd., and 7.34 percent locally owned; and City Savings and Investment Bank, Ltd., which is 52 percent owned by Bank Industry Malaysia Berhad, 37 percent locally, and 11 percent foreign-owned.

In addition to the presence of banks, a number of other (South African affiliated) private foreign banks are also present in Namibia, including ABN (a Dutch bank) and HSBC, both of which have shares in the Commercial Bank of Namibia.

Stock Market

The Namibia Stock Exchange began operating in October 1992. It is regulated by the Stock Exchanges Control Act and overseen by the registrar of financial institutions. Currently, it lists 30 companies and continues to grow. It provides an alternative means of raising cash for Namibian companies. In terms of market capitalization, the top five companies are Namibia Minerals Corp., Namibia Breweries, CIC Holding, Ltd., Ocean Diamond Mining, and Pep Namibia Holding. The exchange is in the process of establishing an unlisted securities market authority, which will manage a separate trading system for shares of companies that do not meet the stringent requirements for a full board listing on the stock exchange. The nonprofit Namibian Stock Exchange Association is the custodian of the licence to operate the stock exchange. This body is comprised of 37 associate members (representing banks, listed companies, investment institutions, etc.) who sponsored the establishment of the exchange by donating 10,000 Namibia dollars each.

The self-regulated Namibian Stock Exchange owes most of its activity to dual listings with the Johannesburg Stock Exchange. Because of dual listings, the Namibian Stock Exchange has a market capitaliza-tion of about 20 billion Namibia dollars, the second largest in Africa after South Africa. Local trading is light, although some local companies are listed.

There are no restrictions on foreign investment.

Insurance Industry

The insurance industry was established in 1942. The registrar of financial institutions regulates the industry. The six insurance companies in Namibia are Old Mutal, Sanlam, Metropolitan Life, Fedlife, Namlife, and SWABOU. These insurance companies provide life, health, and investment insurance. Due to restrictions on foreign ownership in Namibia's insurance industry, there are no foreign-owned insurance companies.

Other Finance Programs

Namibia is eligible for financial transactions with both OPIC and the U.S. Export-Import Bank. Namibia is a member of MIGA and is eligible for MIGA guarantees and technical assistance. Namibia is also eligible for International Finance Corporation investments, both loan and equity. The International Finance Corporation currently has three operations in Namibia.

U.S. Department of Commerce, International Trade Administration

NIGER

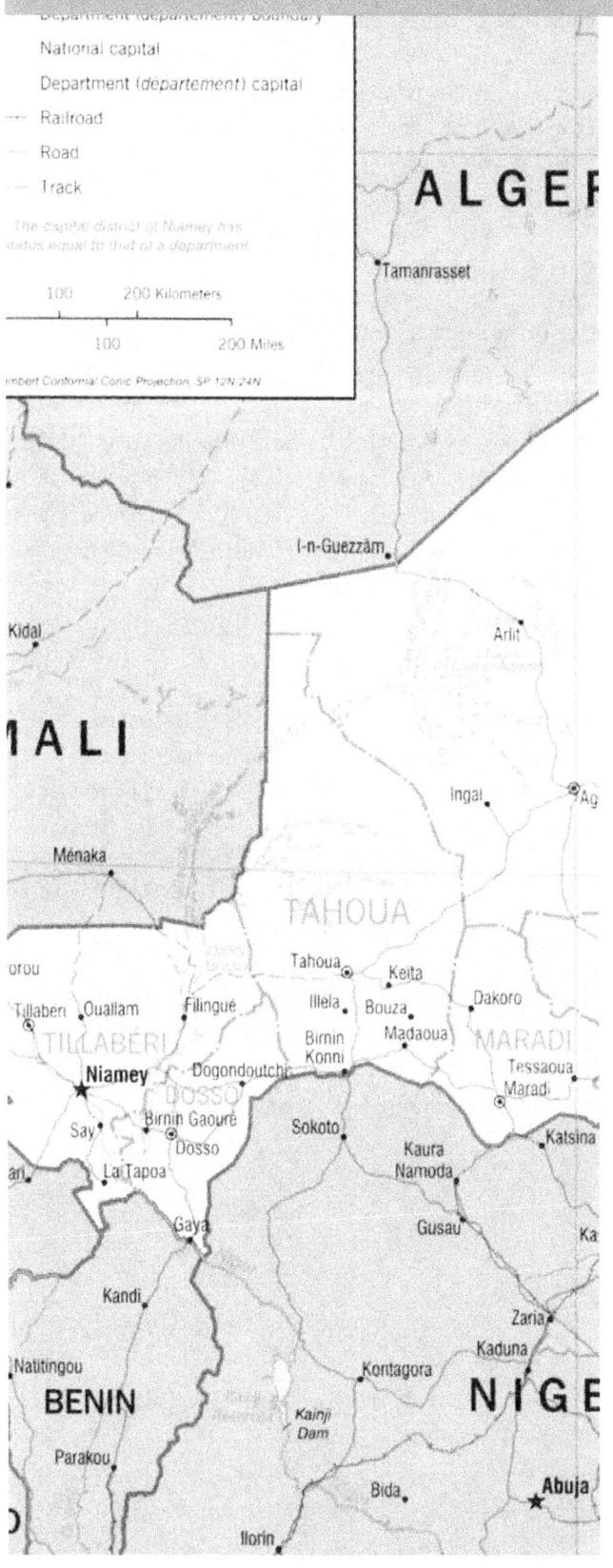

National capital
Department (*département*) capital
--- Railroad
--- Road
--- Track

*The capital district of Niamey has
status equal to that of a department.*

100   200 Kilometers

100   200 Miles

mbert Conformal Conic Projection, SP 12N/24N

Banking Infrastructure

Niger's banking system is governed by the BCEAO. Niger, along with seven other franc zone nations, is a member of the WAEMU. Other member countries are Benin, Burkina Faso, Guinea-Bissau, Ivory Coast, Mali, Senegal, and Togo.

WAEMU established the BCEAO, which issued the CFA franc, the unit of currency for the member states, and established policies governing interest rates. BCEAO banking supervision, strengthened by the role of the WAEMU Banking Commission, has enhanced the enforcement and regulatory provisions of the banking system. BCEAO also has the power to monitor other financial institutions.

While the government's financial policies do not limit the free flow of capital, the private banking sector is small and conservative. It has an exchange system that is free of restrictions on payments and transfers. Investment capital and earnings — dividends, interest, loan and lease payments, royalties, and fees — can be transferred to and from Niger through France. Because several banks have closed in recent years, the remaining ones have tightened their lending criteria. Generally, only well-established businesses obtain bank credit, and the cost of credit is high. Banks in Niger offer only a limited array of financial instruments: letters of credit and short- and long-term loans.

The banking system in Niger consists primarily of two medium-sized local banks — Banque Internationale pour l'Afrique and Société Nigerienne de Banque — and three small commercial banks: Bank of Africa, Banque Islamique du Niger pour le Commerce et l'Investissement, and Ecobank (which opened in July 1999).

Banque Internationale, with a share capital of 2.8 billion CFA francs, has a large international network in Africa and Europe (with offices in Brussels, Paris, and London). The bank's 1998 balance sheet totaled 40.6

billion CFA francs (approximately $58 million). Its customers range from big industrial, commercial, and agricultural companies to small and medium-sized companies, and it has offices throughout the country. It is the local powerhouse, with 45 percent of the banking market and formal connections with the French banking system. The majority of its customers are from large corporations.

Société Nigerienne has a large international network. Its 1999 balance sheet totaled 30.5 billion CFA francs (approximately $43.5 million). It has offices based in Maradi, Zinder, Tahoua, and Arlit, with a broad clientele in all sectors. Its main customers are small enterprises, distributors, insurance companies, manufacturing and mining industries, water, electricity, and petroleum companies, transportation companies, construction and agriculture companies, NGOs, and donor-funded development projects. Its market strategy of cash availability focuses on its network of smaller clients. By creating a loan guarantee development program for microenterprises, it has discovered a lucrative position within the banking sector.

Ecobank is the newest bank to establish a presence in Niger. It has a reasonable international network (through Groupe Bancaire Privée /Ecobank Transnational, Inc., a holding company based in Lomé, Togo) and it also has 42 branches throughout West Africa. Ecobank's main customers include businesspeople, NGOs, international organizations, development projects, some local companies, and households. It attempts to attract regional traders who can benefit from electronic fund transfers, as opposed to more risky cross-border courier services.

Bank of Africa has a large international network in Africa and Europe. Its initial market strategy attempted to gain the trust of large organizations and enterprises. This plan failed, because Niger's client base was too small to support another bank. Therefore, it broadened its strategy to include small and medium-sized companies, projects, NGOs, international organizations, businesses, and private individuals.

Banque Islamique, established in Niger in 1997, is a member of Daral Maal Islammi Group. The bank's share capital equals $2.6 million (1.8 billion CFA francs), with a balance sheet of $8.6 million (6 million CFA francs). The shareholders include Dual Maal Islammi Group (with 33.15 percent), Islamic Development Bank (with 33.15 percent), and OSEM Niger (with 34.7 percent). The bank's major correspondent partners are Trust Bank, Citibank, ABN Amro, and UBAF (Union de Banques Arabes et Françaises). Banque Islamique's main customers include industrial and commercial businesses, but it does not have a clearly defined marketing strategy.

Stock Market

Niger is a member of the Bourse Régionale des Valeurs Mobilières, a regional stock market located in Abidjan, Ivory Coast. Established in 1996, this regional stock market became active in the last three months of 1998. The exchange links Niger with the other French-speaking member countries of the West African Economic and Monetary Union: Benin, Burkina Faso, Guinea-Bissau, Ivory Coast, Mali, Senegal, and Togo.

Insurance Industry

Niger has three insurance companies established since independence in 1960. The insurance industry is regulated by the Ministry of Finance, and all types of insurance are available in Niger. Foreign direct investments are not restricted in this industry.

Other Finance Programs

Niger is eligible for U.S. Export-Import Bank programs and OPIC programs. Niger is not a member of MIGA. While Niger is eligible for OPIC programs, OPIC has not been involved in any investment to date.

NIGERIA

Nigeria

International boundary	◉ State capital
State boundary	---- Railroad
National capital	---- Road

100   200 Kilometers

100   200 Miles

Lambert Conformal Conic Projection, SP 8N 32N

Banking Infrastructure

Nigeria's first bank, the African Banking Corporation, was established in 1892. Banking legislation did not exist until 1952, when the government established ordinance standards, required reserve funds, established bank examinations, and provided assistance to indigenous banks.

The Nigerian financial system is comprised of bank and nonbank financial institutions that are regulated by a number of government entities, including the Ministry of Finance, the Central Bank of Nigeria, the Nigeria Deposit Insurance Corporation, the Securities and Exchange Commission, the National Insurance Commission, the Federal Mortgage Bank of Nigeria, and the National Board for Community Banks.

In 1957, the Central Bank of Nigeria was established. It began operations in 1959, and became independent of the federal government in 1968. The central bank is at the apex of the banking system and has primary responsibility for formulating and monitoring compliance with monetary, credit, and foreign exchange policies. Any person desiring to undertake banking and other financial business in Nigeria must apply in writing to the Central Bank of Nigeria for a grant of license and supply prescribed documents with the application.

The Nigerian banking system is patterned along British lines. Most banks in Nigeria, however, fall into one of three categories: commercial, merchant, or industrial banks. There are more than a hundred banks, with branches all over the country. Licenses are being granted to mortgage and building societies operating along British lines. As of 2001, there were 90 banks in Nigeria, including 57 commercial and 33 merchant banks.

Commercial Banks. The first commercial bank was established in Nigeria in 1892. Commercial banks perform three major functions: acceptance of deposits, granting of loans, and the operation of the payment

45

and settlement mechanism. The number of commercial banks and their branches operating in Nigeria were 2,402 in 1996. Many banks and branches have closed since then, but the commercial banks still continue to dominate the banking sector.

Merchant Banks. Merchant banks take deposits and cater to the needs of corporate and institutional customers by way of providing medium- and long-term loan financing and engaging in activities such as equipment leasing, loan syndication, debt factoring, and project advisers to clients sourcing funds in the market. The first merchant bank in Nigeria, Nigerian Acceptance, Ltd., started operations in 1960. By the end of 1996, there were 51 merchant banks with 147 branches.

Stock Market

The Nigerian (Lagos) Stock Exchange, which commenced business in 1961, is principally a primary capital market and is open to participation by foreign nationals. The Nigerian Capital Market is a channel for mobilizing long-term funds. The main institutions in the market include: the Securities and Exchange Commission, which is at the apex and serves as the regulatory authority of the market; the Lagos Stock Exchange; the issuing houses; and the stock brokage firms. The capital market is classified into primary and secondary segments.

To encourage small as well as large-scale enterprises to gain access to public listing, the exchange operates the main exchange for relatively large enterprise and the Second-Securities Market, where listing requirements are less stringent, for small and medium-scale enterprises.

The exchange is open to foreign participation. Foreign nationals cannot belong to the governing body of the Stock Exchange, since it currently operates as a quasi-governmental organization under the jurisdiction of the Ministry of Trade.

Insurance Industry

Prior to 1992, the Ministry of Finance licensed and supervised insurance companies in Nigeria. In 1997, the National Insurance Commission was established, replacing the National Insurance Supervisory Board. The commission is charged with effective administration, super-

vision, regulation, and control of the business of insurance in Nigeria. Its specific functions include the establishment of standards for the conduct of insurance business, protection of insurance policy holders, and establishment of a bureau to which complaints may be submitted against insurance companies and their intermediaries by members of the public. It ensures adequate capitalization and reserve, good management, high technical expertise, and judicious fund placement in the insurance industry.

The insurance companies consist of life and nonlife insurers, as well as those which engage in both activities, and reinsurance firms. They mobilize relatively long-term funds and act as financial intermediaries. Their investments are mainly in government securities and the mortgage industry. The Nigerian insurance industry has grown tremendously in recent years. There were 187 insurance companies operating in the country in 1996.

Other Finance Programs

Nigeria is now eligible for U.S. Export-Import Bank medium-term financing in the private sector, which will enable Nigerian businesses to buy U.S. capital equipment to build infrastructure. The bank opened for business in Nigeria in August 1999, with a $100 million pilot program for short-term insurance in the private sector.

In the past, the U.S. Export-Import Bank and its insurance affiliate, the Foreign Credit Insurance Association, financed and insured a number of projects in Nigeria. However, in 1992, it adopted a more restrictive policy toward public- and private-sector projects in Nigeria.

The African Development Bank grants export stimulation loans to finance certain operations of exporting companies. It channels these loans through the Central Bank of Nigeria to the Nigerian Export-Import Bank, the National Economic Reconstruction Fund, and licensed exporting banks. The Nigerian Export-Import Bank became operational in January 1991. Nigeria is a member of MIGA.

U.S. Department of Commerce, International Trade Administration

SENEGAL

Banking Infrastructure

Senegal's banking system is governed by the BCEAO. Senegal, along with seven other franc zone nations, is a member of the WAEMU. Other member countries are Benin, Burkina Faso, Guinea-Bissau, Ivory Coast, Mali, Niger, and Togo.

WAEMU established the BCEAO, which issued the CFA franc, the unit of currency for the member states, and established policies governing interest rates. BCEAO banking supervision, strengthened by the role of the WAEMU Banking Commission, has enhanced the enforcement and regulatory provisions of the banking system. BCEAO also has the power to monitor other financial institutions.

Senegal's banks are not required to comply with international accounting standards, but reforms initiated by the BCEAO will change this. Loans are granted based on collateral. A significant portion of commercial bank loans go to large, well-established firms in the food processing and import-export sectors. Lending is mandated neither by law nor by public policy. Regulations limit the percentage of loans that can be granted to shareholders. Bank loan committees monitor lending, while the BCEAO controls credit rates. In general, banks lend to well-established private clients. Some 45 percent of total domestic credit has gone to the private sector over the past two years.

Commercial Banks. Eight commercial banks operate in Senegal, the largest ones are subsidiaries of French banks, many of which have representative offices in the United States. The commercial banking sector is now fully privatized and is considered to have significant surplus liquidity. Five commercial banks have correspondent arrangements with U.S. banks: Crédit Lyonnais Sénégal is affiliated with Crédit Lyonnais of France, which has a representative office in New York; Société Générale de Banques au Sénégal is affiliated with the Société Générale de Banques of France, which has a representative in New York; Banque Internationale pour le Commerce et l'Industrie du Sénégal is affiliated with the Banque Nationale de Paris, which has an office in New York; Banque de l'Habitat du Sénégal, which specializes in housing, also has a branch in New York that targets the growing Senegalese community in the United States; and Caisse Nationale de Crédit Agricole, which provides credit to small-scale rural enterprises, is affiliated with France's Crédit Agricole.

Foreign Banks. Ecobank opened in 1999. Citibank Dakar is the only U.S.-owned bank in Senegal.

Stock Market

Senegal is a member of the Bourse Régionale des Valeurs Mobilières, a regional stock market located in Abidjan, Ivory Coast. Established in 1996, this regional stock market became effective in the last three months of 1998. This exchange links Senegal with the other French-speaking member countries of the West African Economic and Monetary Union: Benin, Burkina Faso, Guinea-Bissau, Ivory Coast, Mali, Niger, and Togo.

Insurance Industry

The Senegalese insurance industry has been established since the colonial period. Nine insurance companies operate in Senegal: Société Nationale d'Assurance au Sénégal (affiliated with AGF France); SONAM; AXA (affiliated with AXA France); La Prevoyance Assurances; La Sécurité Seneglaise; Les Assurances Générales du Sénégal; Alliance; SOSAR; and Illico. The nine insurance companies are regulated by the Ministry of Finance and Economic Affairs. There are no restrictions regarding foreign ownership in the insurance industry. Civil liability is covered by all insurance companies. Illico covers only life insurance. SONAM, the Société Nationale, AXA, and Les Assurances Générales also have life insurance branches.

Other Finance Programs

The U.S. Export-Import Bank is fully off-cover for private-sector projects in Senegal, but in 1998 it opened for medium-term financing in the public sector. The bank is actively seeking new business in Senegal for its guarantee and direct export finance program.

In cooperation with OPIC, Citicorp offers the African Trade Finance Facility, which finances U.S. exports to Africa by purchasing term trade obligations of importers in Africa. It can also confirm letters of credit issued to U.S. exporters. OPIC also supports the Modern Africa Growth and Investment Fund, a $150 million direct investment fund that will invest equity capital in new, expanding, or privatizing companies in various African countries, potentially including Senegal. These funds are intended to support the formation of joint ventures between U.S. firms and firms in sub-Saharan Africa.

The U.S. Department of Agriculture's West Africa Regional GSM-102 Export Credit Guarantee program provides for access to financing for import of wheat, rice, feed grains, vegetable oil, protein meal, and dairy products. The African Development Bank and the World Bank finance projects dealing with infrastructure. Senegal is a member MIGA. In 2000, the International Finance Corporation opened a regional office in Senegal.

48

U.S. Department of Commerce, International Trade Administration

South Africa

Banking Infrastructure

The banking sector in South Africa is regulated by the South Africa Reserve Bank through the Deposit-Taking Institutions Act, which is administered by the registrar of deposit-taking institutions.

The South African Banks Act, which became operative in 1991, exerts legislative control over the banking sector. The regulatory structure of the financial services industry, except banks, is controlled by the Financial Services Board, which is responsible for licenses and exchanges, conducts investigations, reviews new listings and exchange rules, and advises the registrars of financial markets and stock exchanges.

As of January 1998, South Africa had 56 fully licensed institutions and 60 representative offices of foreign banks. None of the banks are state-owned. Despite high interest margins and a 1.2 percent return on assets (equal to that of U.S. banks), South African banks are hampered by high cost ratios and a relatively low 12.1 percent return on equity. The industry is dominated by four large banks: Standard Bank, Amalgamated Banks of South Africa, First National, and Nederlandsche Bank Voor Zuid Afrika, which has operations internationally. Among them, these banks control about 80 percent of total South African banking assets and a similar percentage of outstanding loans. Of the four major banks, Standard Bank appears to have strategically expanded abroad, especially in other African countries.

Commercial Banks. South African commercial banks provide a full range of banking services to all sectors of the retail and corporate markets. Typically, however, they will not make loans (other than overdrafts) of less than $2,000, so this sector of the market is serviced by nonbank lenders.

Foreign banks. Only one U.S. bank, Citibank, has a full commercial banking license. Four other U.S. banks (Banker Trust, Chase, First Union, and Bank of America)

49

have representative offices that focus on corporate rather that individual business. Foreign banks with more than $1 billion in assets may establish branches in South Africa or acquire full ownership of local banks upon approval of the registrar of banks. There is significant cross-share holding between banks, industrial companies, and insurance and other financial services organizations. The over-ranked and relatively sophisticated nature of the market have mitigated against the entry of many foreign banks into the South African market. In addition to Citibank, foreign banks from the United Kingdom, Germany, France, the Netherlands, Taiwan, Greece, and Cyprus operate either through subsidiaries or as investors in local operations. South African financial institutions are going through the same "merger mania" as other such organizations in the United States and Europe. In 2000 and 2001 mergers between large banks, insurance companies, and merchant banks have been consummated, as local firms try to achieve the scale necessary to compete with the international companies coming into their markets.

The following requirements must be met in order for a foreign bank to establish a branch in South Africa:

• The foreign institution should hold net assets of value of at least $1 billion, as certified by auditors and reflected in the audited annual financial statements. This level of assets must have been held for at least 18 months prior to the submission to establish a branch.

• Intangible and "not readily marketable" assets must be excluded from total assets.

• The foreign institution should have a long-term investment grade debt rating from an internationally recognized rating agency.

• Management must be comprised of at least two persons residing in South Africa, one of whom is the chief executive officer.

• The business operations must at all times be covered and supported by a letter of comfort and undertaking issued from the parent company.

• The branch must have its own capital of not less than $10 million, or 8 percent of the amount of risk-weighted assets and other contingent liabilities.

In addition, foreign bank branches are limited in

their business by: (1) being able to only accept deposits from corporations or from individuals with an initial deposit of more than $200,000 and a balance that is maintained at that level or higher at all times; (2) needing to maintain a net open position in foreign currencies of less than 15 percent of net capital and reserves. A foreign bank approved by the registrar of banks may acquire up to 100 percent of the shares of a local bank or hold 100 percent of the capital of a subsidiary established in South Africa. These subsidiaries are treated in precisely the same manner as any other South African bank and are not limited as to the scope of their activities or regulated differently from other local institutions.

Stock Market

The **Johannesburg Stock Exchange** (JSE), sole licensed stock exchange in South Africa, has 55 members, 11 of which are controlled by foreign companies. Merrill Lynch has purchased a controlling interest in a local securities firm. In 1995, the JSE established a restructuring program to bring it into accordance with worldwide technical and regulatory standards. The JSE is promoting greater cooperation among regional stock exchanges to facilitate regional economic integration, cross-border investment, and foreign participation in the market. In 1996, membership was opened to foreign companies under new capital adequacy requirements applicable equally to domestic and foreign participants in the market. Also in 1996, the exchange introduced dual capacity (broker and dealer) trading, negotiated commissions, and a new automated trading system. The JSE expects to have a fully electronic system in place.

Although the JSE ranks 19th worldwide in terms of total capitalization, it still remains less liquid than other major world exchanges due to the closely-held ownership structure among large South African conglomerates and continued foreign exchange controls. Foreign ownership is estimated at 9 percent of total capitalization. At the end of 1999, the JSE listed 668 companies, and its market capitalization was $262.5 billion.

The **Bond Exchange of South Africa** (BESA) was licensed by the Financial Services Board in 1996 as a self-regulatory financial exchange to replace the previous over-the-counter bond market. Foreign companies must incorporate a public company in South Africa or register as an external company under the Companies Act of 1973 to acquire membership as either trading or broker members. All members are required to meet capital adequacy requirements based on European Union guidelines. Several U.S. banks are BESA trading members, including J.P. Morgan, Merrill Lynch, and Morgan Guaranty Trust of New York. The Ministry of Finance recently introduced an auction system for primary issues and appointed 12 primary dealers for the marketing of South African government capital market debt instruments. Two U.S. firms — J.P. Morgan and Merrill Lynch — were among the five foreign companies appointed.

The **South African Futures Exchange** (SAFEX) began operations in 1990 under a license from the registrar of financial markets that authorizes it to regulate the trading of futures and options. It is the only derivatives exchange in South Africa. The exchange offers financial, commodity, and options contracts. Daily trading volume has risen from 200 contracts in 1990 to roughly 40,000 contracts in 1997. Some 96 percent of futures and options traded through SAFEX are based on Johannesburg Stock Exchange equity index futures, with trading volume over twice the value of trades in underlying equities. SAFEX offers membership in two classes, clearing and nonclearing members. Clearing members must be registered financial institutions in South Africa with a minimum net worth of 200 million rand, and must provide a surety to the clearing house of 10 million rand. A nonclearing member must have an initial capital of at least 400,000 rand and satisfy the executive committee that it has entered into a clearing agreement with a clearing member based on that member's careful evaluation of the nonclearing member's financial standing and integrity. To date, two U.S. companies — J.P. Morgan and Merrill Lynch — hold nonclearing memberships in the exchange via local subsidiaries. The U.S. Commodity Futures Trading Commission has prohibited U.S. companies from dealing directly in SAFEX because of concerns regarding the continued narrow ownership structure of JSE-listed companies and the potential for market manipulation.

U.S. participation in the South African securities industry is expanding rapidly. Since 1994, several U.S.

securities companies have obtained memberships in the JSE, BESA, and SAFEX. Many U.S. firms are active in providing underwriting services and arranging asset swaps for South African government and nongovernment institutions. Most do not have permanent representation in South Africa but service the market out of U.S. or European offices. Financial advisory services, including privatization, corporate restructuring, mergers and acquisitions, and foreign placements (including asset swaps) have provided lucrative service-based business for U.S. bank and nonbank financial institutions.

There are no legal prohibitions on foreigners operating in the South African securities industry. Foreign investment in South African equity and debt instruments are not subject to foreign exchange regulations. Due to the liberalization and deregulation of the market, both individual and institutional U.S. investors have increased their presence dramatically.

A restriction on foreign membership in the JSE was lifted in 1996. Several U.S. firms are trading members of the BESA and nonclearing members of SAFEX. Although the Financial Services Board (FSB) is responsible for the coordination of overall regulatory policy affecting financial markets, the JSE, BESA, and SAFEX operate on a self-regulatory basis subject to the provisions of the National Stock Exchange Control Act of 1985. In order to facilitate growth and tighten regulatory oversight, the FSB and the three exchanges have agreed in principle to amalgamate all trading activities in one national exchange.

Insurance Industry

The South African insurance market is regulated by the registrar of insurance. The insurance industry in South Africa is highly developed and consisted of about 93 companies in 1992. Of these, 37 offered exclusively life business, 45 offered general business, while 11 were composites. The life insurance industry is dominated by two mutual organizations, Sanlana and the South African Mutual Assurance Company (Old Mutual).

There are no restrictions on foreign companies that wish to establish an insurance company in South Africa. Foreign companies are subject to the same requirements as local companies. The number of service providers is not limited by any restrictions. Currently, there are no state-owned companies registered with the FSB, which supervises both the long- and short-term insurance services sectors. Under the Insurance Act, insurers have to register as life, home service, or sinking funds for long-term insurance to carry on business.

Long-term insurance business is classified as any life, industrial, funeral, home service, or sinking fund business. Currently, a total of 51 long-term insurers and six reinsurers do business in South Africa. The total premium income at the end of 1996 stood at $10.5 billion, and total value of long-term insurance assets stood at $68.5 billion. The spread of assets has remained relatively constant and is in line with that of the international insurance industry. The past five or so years have seen the South African long-term insurance industry moving toward more transparent and market-based policies.

In 1943, the Insurance Act was amended to permit life insurers to underwrite obligations that a medical aid scheme owes to its members and to enable life insurers to invest in foreign assets. This new long-term insurance act came into force on January 1, 1998. Also, long-term insurers will no longer be required to obtain the supporting comments of the board for any swap applications, on the basis that it is now the responsibility of their directors to ensure that the insurers will be financially sound after the transaction and that all legal requirements will be adhered to. The industry currently has both domestic and foreign insurers and reinsurers. These include Munich Re Group, Old Mutual, Swiss Re, and others. Unit trust schemes and linked product providers have recently become part of the broader long-term industry, thereby increasing competition in the industry.

Short-term insurance business means insurance in the form of an engineering policy, motor policy, guarantee policy, accident and health policy, property, transportation, and other combinations of the above. As of March 1997, there were a total of 62 short-term insurers, 111 Lloyd's agents, as well as 950 credit agencies in South Africa adding up to a grand total of 1,123 short-term insurers and intermediaries in the country. Short-term insurers and their agents have to be registered to transact in the short-term insurance business. Recently,

there has been an increase in the number of foreign investors seeking advice on the registration of short-term insurers in South Africa.

Other Finance Programs

The U.S. Export-Import Bank and the U.S. Trade and Development Agency offer their programs to support U.S. trade and investment activities in South Africa. The South African government has a number of development agencies that provide project financing. With the lifting of international sanctions against South Africa, a number of multilateral lending agencies have made their financing programs available to projects in South Africa.

South Africa is a member of MIGA. OPIC insurance is available for South Africa.

U.S. Department of Commerce, International Trade Administration

TANZANIA

Banking Infrastructure

After nearly 25 years of government monopoly, the Tanzanian government passed legislation in August 1991 that allowed private banks back into Tanzania. The central bank, Bank of Tanzania, is responsible for the supervision of banks and other financial institutions. As of June 1998, several private banks have registered with the Bank of Tanzania. The National Bank of Commerce, which used to account for over 75 percent of the country's transactions, was split into the National Bank of Commerce and the National Microfinance Bank in 1997. Reform in the banking sector is continuing, with plans to privatize the National Bank of Commerce and the National Microfinance Bank. There are also plans for the privatization of the People's Bank of Zanzibar, which operates as a quasi-central bank to the Zanzibar government. The Co-operative and Rural Development Bank, which operates primarily in rural areas and provides agricultural financing, is the last of the most significant commercial banks that remain under government control. It will eventually be privatized.

Since 1996, the financial sector has expanded significantly. In June 1998, the sector was comprised of 19 licensed commercial banks (17 operating), nine non-bank financial institutions, 105 foreign exchange bureaus, and a number of information intermediaries such as the Savings and Credit Cooperatives Societies. The six largest banks — National Bank of Commerce, the Co-operative Rural and Development Bank, Citibank, National Microfinance, Standard Chartered, and Stanbic Bank Tanzania — hold 90 percent of all assets.

The Bank of Commerce has correspondent arrangements with Chase Manhattan, Morgan Trust Guaranty, and Citibank. Foreign banks like Trust Bank, Ltd., and Citibank have similar correspondent arrangements with U.S. banks. Citibank is the only U. S. bank currently operating in Tanzania. Tanzania Postal Bank has a money transfer arrangement with Western Union

53

International of the United States. The Postal Express Tanzania, Ltd., Bank of Tanzania (Central Bank) Dar es Salaam, National Bank of Commerce, Maritime Forwards Std., and the Co-operative and Rural Development Airline and Tour Operations Bank are clearing banks and forwarding agents.

The Bank of Commerce, Microfinance Bank, Co-operative and Rural Development Bank, Stanbic Bank, and Standard Chartered provide financial resources for exports and to qualified firms. The availability of local financing is limited. Current policies are geared to facilitating the free flow of financial resources and credit is allocated on market terms, but it has not been economical to borrow from local sources due to high interest rates and lower producer prices. There are no laws or regulations in Tanzania that authorize private firms to adopt restrictive measures on foreign participation in their firms.

Stock Market

For three decades after its independence in 1961, Tanzania followed a socialist, state-owned economic model. In 1994, the Capital Development and Markets Authority was established and the first stock exchange was opened in Dar es Salaam in March 1998. The Dar es Salaam Stock Exchange had two private companies listed for share floatation by July 1998. Several other companies, including a number of private firms and formerly government-owned firms, are contemplating registering for share floatation in the near future.

Insurance Industry

The insurance sector is regulated by the Insurance Act of 1996. The Insurance Act grants the president the authority to establish a National Reinsurance Corporation in which all Tanzanian insurers would be required to reinsure a portion of their insurance, but this provision has not been implemented. The commissioner for insurance is responsible for general administration of the act; a deputy commissioner is responsible for its administration in Zanzibar. The act brought an end to the government monopoly in insurance services, which had existed since 1967.

The National Insurance Company is a quasi-govern-

mental organization scheduled to be privatized, although no time frame has been established. Responsibility for the insurance sector rests with the Insurance Supervisory Department within the Ministry of Finance. A National Insurance Board, appointed by the minister of finance, has responsibility for advising and assisting the insurance commissioner independent of the policy-making role, which will be maintained by the Department of Finance.

Insurance services are provided by 11 registered insurance companies in Tanzania. Reinsurance services are not currently available in Tanzania. As a consequence, all reinsurance is placed outside Tanzania, either with regional reinsurance entities or with private reinsurers. A quasi-governmental insurance company provides cover against loss, damage, and destruction, but does not provide financing for exports or imports.

Other Finance Programs

OPIC insurance is available to Tanzania. U.S. Export-Import Bank financing is only available for privately owned companies. Project financing is available from the Tanzania Development Finance Company, Ltd., Tanzania Investment Bank, Tanzania Venture Capital Fund, East African Development Bank, African Development Bank, the International Bank for Reconstruction and Development, International Development Agency, and the International Finance Corporation. Tanzania is a member of MIGA.

U.S. Department of Commerce, International Trade Administration

T OGO

Banking Infrastructure

Togo's banking system is governed by the BCEAO. Togo, along with seven other franc zone nations, is a member of the WAEMU. Other member countries are Benin, Burkina Faso, Guinea-Bissau, Ivory Coast, Mali, Niger, and Senegal.

WAEMU established the BCEAO, which issued the CFA franc, the unit of currency for the member states, and established policies governing interest rates. BCEAO banking supervision, strengthened by the role of the WAEMU Banking Commission, has enhanced the enforcement and regulatory provisions of the banking system. BCEAO also has the power to monitor other financial institutions.

Togo's banking system is well-developed due to its traditional reputation as a regional trading center. The major commercial banks are Union Togolaise de Banque, Banque Togolaise pour le Commerce et l'Industrie, Ecobank, and the Banque Togolaise de Développement. All major banks in Togo have correspondent relationships with U.S. banks.

The Togolese banks have generally been in better financial conditions than their counterparts in other CFA franc zone countries, but they were weakened by the economic crisis. A long general strike in 1992–1993 and an attendant drop in commercial activity, has affected the banks negatively. The central bank tightened controls on capital outflows not directly tied to business transactions in 1991, but transfers for business-related purposes are still routinely granted.

Stock Market

Togo is a member of the Bourse Régionale des Valeurs Mobilières, a regional stock market located in Abidjan, Ivory Coast. Established in 1996, this regional stock market became effective in the last three months of 1998. This exchange links Togo with the other French-speaking member countries of the West African

Economic and Monetary Union: Benin, Burkina Faso, Guinea-Bissau, Ivory Coast, Mali, Niger, and Senegal.

Insurance Industry

Information covering Togo's insurance industry is not available.

Other Finance Programs

OPIC investment insurance is available for American investors in Togo. In the past, OPIC has played an active role in promoting foreign investment in Togo.

Investment insurance is also available through MIGA. Multilateral institutions involved in funding projects in Togo include the African Development Bank, the ECOW-AS Fund, the West African Development Bank, and the World Bank. U.S. Export-Import Bank short-term financing is available to publicly-owned companies and for specially financed transactions.

U.S. Department of Commerce, International Trade Administration

UGANDA

Banking Infrastructure

Uganda's banking system is supervised by the central bank, the Bank of Uganda. In the 1970s, the government of Uganda nationalized all banks. Private ownership returned in 1987. Since 1996, Bank of Uganda has controlled currency issues and foreign exchange reserves while the government-owned Uganda Commercial Bank dominates the commercial sector. The state-owned Uganda Development Bank, aided by the World Bank, administers international and development loans made to Uganda while the East African Development Bank, jointly owned by Uganda, Tanzania, and Kenya, deals with development finance.

Finance is a major issue in Uganda. To promote and maintain a sound and reputable financial sector, the Bank of Uganda has placed a moratorium on the licensing of banks and credit institutions offering banking services in urban areas. Banks are generally weak and hesitant to loan. (For example, in September 1998 the central bank closed three banks; two major banks were closed in 1999). While general financing is available through commercial banks and credit institutions, the interest rate spread over deposit rate is extremely high. Time periods for loan payments are extremely short. There is a limited interbank lending market, in which credit quality is a major concern.

There are both foreign-owned and domestic banks established in Uganda. Domestic banks tend to be less well-capitalized than foreign banks. Ugandan banks have correspondence with the following U.S. banks: Citibank, Chemical Bank, Barclays, Chase Manhattan Bank, Bankers Trust, and Standard Chartered Bank.

Commercial Banks. Uganda has 18 commercial banks and two development banks. The Uganda Commercial Bank has the largest number of branches. Commercial banks can, and sometimes do, sell Treasury bills to the central bank to obtain reserves, though this is costly because the central bank demands a discount from the price the holder could get in the small secondary mar-

57

ket. Commercial lending is limited, because private-sector borrowers who are good credit risks are few. Interest rates for loans are about 20 percent. Reserve requirements on bank deposits are 25 percent. The Ugandan shilling has a floating exchange rate. No exchange controls exist.

Stock Market

The Uganda Securities Exchange was inaugurated in 1997. The Capital Markets Authority, the regulatory body, has licensed eight brokers. Participants, however, are still preparing for an actual exchange to evolve. No publicly traded shares exist yet, and the Capital Markets Authority serves more as a promoter than a regulator at this stage. Privatization of state enterprises is expected to result in public sales of shares, which could then be traded on the stock exchange. The Capital Markets Authority is also considering allowing Treasury bills to be traded on the exchange. That might help the tiny secondary market in Treasury bills to grow, since it would make the secondary market more visible and accessible to the public. A draft law authorizing unit trusts is currently under review. Once enacted, such a law will enable money market mutual funds and other investment vehicles to be established.

Insurance Industry

Information on Uganda's insurance industry is not available.

Other Finance Programs

The U.S. Export-Import Bank is open in Uganda for short- to medium-term loans. OPIC is also open and can provide political risk insurance as well as financing for projects. Multilateral institutions active in Uganda include the World Bank and the African Development Bank, as well as several European institutions. Uganda is a member of MIGA.

U.S. Department of Commerce, International Trade Administration

ZAMBIA

Banking Infrastructure

Zambia's banking sector is supervised by the central bank, the Bank of Zambia, which reports to the Ministry of Finance.

Commercial Banks. Zambia has a commercial banking sector composed of private international banks, private domestic banks, and quasi-governmental banks. Of the 15 active banks, six are foreign-owned subsidiaries, seven are owned by local investors, one is owned by India, and one by the Zambian government.

State-owned Financial Institutions. Through the government's holding company, Zambia Industrial and Mining Corporation, the government owns 99.8 percent of the Zambia National Commercial Bank. There are two development banks, the Development Bank of Zambia and the Lima Bank. Other state-owned financial institutions include the Zambia State Insurance Corporation, the Zambia National Building Society, and the Zambia Export and Import Bank, Ltd. (which was established in early 1988).

Foreign Banks. The Credit Bank of Africa, a new bank, is listed but not well-known. Barclays, Citibank, ANZ, Meridien BIAO, and Standard Chartered have all set up subsidiaries in Lusaka.

With interest rates in excess of 40 percent (the prime rate), foreign financing remains prohibitively high. With the abolishment of exchange controls any investor can borrow for investing in Zambia, but certain financial institutions will not provide loans to investors deemed as nonresidents unless a wholly owned Zambian company participates in the business.

Local Banks. Domestic financing is in short supply except for export-oriented production. Interest rates are still high, which makes medium- or long-term borrowing unfeasible. Short-term borrowing is available but expensive. Many businesses either self-finance or seek financing in hard currency outside the country. A letter of credit is the most common method of payment used for

59

Zambian imports. In general, companies find it very difficult to finance their own imports and seek credit arrangements. But they make a very careful check of the bona fides and finances of Zambian companies before doing so. Delinquent payments to suppliers are a common problem in Zambia.

Stock Market

The Lusaka Stock Exchange was established in February 1994. The exchange is regulated by the Securities and Exchange Commission. The exchange currently transacts nine listed and six unlisted securities. The number of securities traded on the exchange is expected to increase as up to 150 state enterprises are privatized over the next few years and a number of privately held companies convert to public ownership and issue shares on the market. Treasury bills and other government bonds will also be traded on the exchange. There are no restrictions on foreign investment, and foreigners may invest on the stock exchange on similar terms as Zambians.

Insurance Industry

The insurance industry is controlled by the Zambia State Insurance Corporation. Further information on Zambia's insurance industry is not available.

Other Finance Programs

The U.S. Export-Import Bank is currently open only for specially financed transactions and is off-cover for other programs in Zambia. OPIC offers project financing, political risk insurance, and investor services in Zambia. The International Finance Corporation and the Commonwealth Development Corporation both offer financing for projects in Zambia. The availability of project financing, particularly for export-oriented projects, is improving. Besides bilateral and multilateral government agencies, commercial banks and venture capital funds are playing increasing roles. Both the United States and the European Union have established enterprise development funds that encompass Zambia. Zawbia is a member of MIGA.

Banking Infrastructure

Zimbabwe's central bank, the Reserve Bank of Zimbabwe, regulates the banking sector and carefully monitors the establishment of new banks. The banking sector is well-diversified, with banks offering a full range of services. Zimbabwe's banking sector is more active than that in any other sub-Saharan nation except South Africa, but still needs to modernize as the country liberalizes.

The Reserve Bank plays a key role in formulating and administering the government's monetary policy. The Reserve Bank acts as a banker to the government, issues currency and government loans, controls foreign reserves, serves as a banker to the country's financial institutions, acts as a lender of last resort to commercial banks, administers the exchange control regulations, and handles the sale of gold and silver.

The Reserve Bank, the commercial banks, the merchant banks, the Post Office Savings Bank, and the discount houses make up what is known as the monetary banking sector. The discount houses act as intermediaries between the Reserve Bank and the rest of the financial sector:

• commercial banks, which are the largest subsector;

• acceptance houses and merchant banks, whose main function is to finance trade, underwrite share offerings of finance houses, which usually lend directly to consumers;

• building societies, which finance real estate transactions;

• the Post Office Savings Bank, which is a savings bank that invests only in government paper; and

• the development banks, which are government-owned and primarily finance industry.

The largest local banks are Zimbabwe Banking Corporation, First Merchant Bank of Zimbabwe, and Merchant Bank of Central Africa. Major Western banks such as Standard Chartered, Barclays, NZ Grindlays, and Standard Bank operate in Zimbabwe.

Zimbabwe banks have correspondent arrangements with the following U.S. banks: Federal Bank of New York, Bankers Trust, Chase Manhattan, Barclays Bank, Standard Chartered Bank, Citibank, and Irving Trust.

Commercial Banks. There are seven operating commercial banks. Many commercial banks are foreign owned, though the local affiliates enjoy a substantial measure of autonomy from their parent companies. The largest locally owned bank, Zimbabwe Banking Corporation, Ltd., in which the government holds a controlling interest, maintains correspondent arrangements with over 300 banks in 80 countries. Zimbabwe's largest banking group, the Standard Chartered Bank Zimbabwe, Ltd., was the first financial institution to open an office in Zimbabwe, in 1892.

Discount Houses. There are six operating discount houses that act as intermediaries between the Reserve Bank and the financial sector. They are involved in accepting money at call from other banking institutions and provide a short-term market for the purchase and sale of public sector stocks, municipal stock, negotiable certificates of deposit, and bankers acceptances.

Merchant Banks. A secondary financial structure came into being as a result of the commercial banks being forced to increase domestic assets and to reinvest in the country. The primary role of merchant banks is trade financing, through the acceptance of bills of exchange. They provide advice and services relating to all privatization and management buyouts for both listed and unlisted companies, as well as handling and underwriting rights issues and other new issues or the placing of equity-based securities. Two of the nine merchant banks, Standard Chartered Merchant Bank Zimbabwe, Ltd., and Syfrets Merchant Bank, Ltd., are subsidiaries of Standard Chartered Merchant Bank Overseas, Ltd., and Zimbabwe Banking Corporation, Ltd., respectively.

Stock Market

The Zimbabwe Stock Exchange has been trading since 1946, although a stock exchange in one form or another was functioning as far back as the late 1800s. The exchange is governed by the Stock Exchange Act. Zimbabwe's stock market is small, but active, with 65 companies listed. Trading is carried out through stockbrokers, and official price lists are published daily in the national press. Securities of 54 companies incorporated in Zimbabwe are listed, as are true locally registered stocks of government, municipal, and statutory bodies. No prior Exchange Control approval is necessary for a foreign investor to participate on the Zimbabwe Stock Exchange. Foreigners are free to buy and sell stocks, provided foreign funds are utilized for such acquisitions. Foreign holdings of shares are limited to 40 percent of total equity of a company, and a single investor can only acquire a maximum of 10 percent of the shares on offer. Foreign investors are still not permitted to purchase from the secondary market.

The government offers capital gains incentives for individuals to make portfolio investments in the stock exchange. In addition to corporate shares, government and municipal bonds are traded on the Zimbabwe Stock Exchange.

Insurance Industry

The insurance industry is regulated by the Insurance Act, and there is a commissioner for insurance, supervised by the Ministry of Finance and Economic Development. Several insurance companies do business in Zimbabwe, most of them affiliates of companies with offices abroad. The U.S. insurance company, AIG, is also established there. The biggest insurance company, Old Mutual, is locally incorporated. All insurance companies and pension and provident funds are required to place 55 percent of their investments in government stock and local authority stocks. There are more than 50 registered insurance companies operating in the life and nonlife fields.

Other Finance Programs

U.S. Export-Import Bank programs are available to exporters to finance exports to Zimbabwe. In April 1999, the U.S. government and the government of Zimbabwe concluded an updated OPIC agreement. OPIC is interested in participating in and coordinating the financial structuring of new ventures in Zimbabwe, as are the World Bank-affiliated International Finance

U.S. Department of Commerce, International Trade Administration

Corporation and the European Investment Bank. The Industrial Development Corporation, government-owned holding company is primarily involved in the manufacturing sector and is interested in joint ventures with foreign firms. The Zimbabwe Development Corporation is a similar quasi-governmental organization, whose objectives are to invest government funds in profit-making commercial enterprises, which often include joint ventures with both local and foreign firms. Zimbabwe was accepted as a member of MIGA in September 1989.

APPENDIX A: EXPORT-IMPORT BANK OF THE UNITED STATES

The Export-Import Bank of the United States (Ex-Im Bank) helps the private sector to create and maintain U.S. jobs by financing exports of the nation's goods and services. To accomplish this mission, the bank offers a variety of loan, guarantee, and insurance programs to support transactions that would not be awarded to U.S. companies without the bank's assistance.

The bank, established in 1934, operates as an independent agency of the U.S. government under the authority of the Export-Import Bank Act of 1945, as amended (12 U.S.C. 635 et seq.). Its board of directors consists of a president and chairman, a first vice president and vice chairman, and three other directors, all of whom are appointed by the president of the United States with the advice and consent of the Senate.

The Ex-Im Bank's mission is to help American exporters meet government-supported financing competition from other countries, so that U.S. exports can compete for overseas business on the basis of price, performance, and service. The bank also fills gaps in the availability of commercial financing for creditworthy export transactions.

The Ex-Im Bank is required to find a reasonable assurance of repayment for each transaction it supports. Its legislation requires it to meet the financing terms of competitor export credit agencies, but not to compete with commercial lenders. Legislation restricts the bank's operation in some countries and its support for military goods and services.

The Ex-Im Bank is authorized to have outstanding, at any one time, loans, guarantees, and insurance in aggregate amount not in excess of $75 billion. It supports U.S. exporters through a range of diverse programs, which are offered under four broad categories of export financing:

- **working capital guarantees,** provided to lenders so that they can provide creditworthy small and medium-sized exporters with working capital they need to buy, build, or assemble products for export sale;

- **export credit insurance,** which protects exporters and lenders against both the commercial and political risks of a foreign buyer defaulting on payment;

- **loan guarantees,** which encourage sales to creditworthy foreign buyers by providing private sector lenders in medium- and long-term transactions with Ex-Im Bank guarantees against the political and commercial risks of non-payment; and

- **direct loans** made to provide foreign buyers with competitive, fixed-rate medium- or long-term financing from the Ex-Im Bank for their purchases from U.S. exporters.

The Ex-Im Bank has initiated several new programs to broaden the range of customers and types of exporters it supports. It has also expanded its capabilities in the area of limited recourse project finance and has adopted a policy of matching foreign tied-aid credits to ensure that U.S. exporters do not lose sales in critical emerging markets. In order to make its programs more readily available, the Ex-Im Bank works closely with many state and local governments in its City/State Partners Program.

The Export-Import Bank operates six regional offices. They are located in New York, Miami, Chicago, Houston, Los Angeles, and Washington, D.C. Satellite office are located in San Jose, Calif., and Newport Beach, Calif.

For further information, contact the Export-Import Bank, Business Development Office, 811 Vermont Avenue N.W., Washington, DC 20571; telephone (202) 565-3900 or, toll-free, (800) 565-EXIM. On the Internet, *www.exim.gov.*

(Text from *U.S. Government Manual,* 2001–2002 edition.)

Availability of Export-Import Bank Programs in Sub-Saharan Africa, by Country

Country	Type of loan Short-term	Medium-term	Long-term	Open for specially financed transactions?
Angola				yes
Benin	public and private	public and private		yes
Botswana	public and private	public and private	public and private	yes
Burkina Faso	public* and private	private	private	yes
Cameroon	public* and private	private		yes
Congo (Democratic Republic of)				yes
Congo				yes
Ethiopia				yes
Gabon	public and private	public and private	public and private	yes
Gambia	public* and private	private		yes
Ghana	public and private	public and private	public and private	yes
Guinea	private*			yes
Guinea-Bissau				yes
Ivory Coast	private	private	private	yes
Kenya	public and private	public and private		yes
Malawi	public* and private*			yes
Mauritania	public* and private*			yes
Mozambique	private	private	private	yes
Namibia	public and private	public and private	public and private	yes
Niger	private	private		yes
Nigeria	private	private		yes
Senegal	public and private	public and private	public and private	yes
South Africa	public and private	public and private	public and private	yes
Tanzania	private	private		yes
Togo	public*			yes
Uganda	public and private	public and private		yes
Zambia				yes
Zimbabwe				yes

*Sectors open under the bank's Short-Term Africa Pilot Program.

Source: Export-Import Bank of the United States. For upates, consult the bank's Web site *at www.exim.gov*, under "Country Information," or call (800) 565-3946, ext. 3900.

Definitions of terms used in table
on page 66:

Short-term loans: loans for consumables, raw materials, and small capital goods; repayment term of up to 360 days.

Medium-term loans: loans for capital goods and/or services, with a repayment term of up to seven years (maximum two years for disbursement, plus five years for repayment).

Long-term loans: loans for capital goods and/or services, with repayment terms of up to seven years.

Public sector: entities at least 50 percent owned by a government.

Private sector: privately-owned companies, financial instructions, and other entities less than 50 percent owned by a government.

Specially financed transactions: these include project finance transactions (projects without full recourse to established obligor or guarantor), asset-based aircraft leases or sales, arrangements offering access to foreign exchange, third-country obligors or guarantors, borrowers with access to international capital markets, etc.

APPENDIX B: MULTILATERAL INVESTMENT GUARANTEE AGENCY

The Multilateral Investment Guarantee Agency (MIGA) was created in 1988 as a member of the World Bank Group to promote foreign direct investment into emerging economies to improve people's lives and reduce poverty. MIGA fulfills this mandate and contributes to development by offering political risk insurance (guarantees) to investors and lenders, and by helping developing countries attract and retain private investment.

MIGA is led in its mission by four guiding principles:

• focusing on clients — serving investors, lenders, and host country governments by supporting private enterprise and promoting foreign investment;

• engaging in partnerships — working with other insurers, government agencies, and international organizations to ensure complementarity of services and approach;

• promoting developmental impact — striving to improve the lives of people in emerging economies, consistent with the goals of host countries and sound business, environmental, and social principles;

• ensuring financial soundness — balancing developmental goals and financial objectives through prudent underwriting and sound risk management.

MIGA membership, which currently stands at 154, is open to all World Bank members. The agency has a capital stock of SDR [Special Drawing Rights] 1 billion. In March 1999, MIGA's Council of Governors adopted a resolution for a capital increase of approximately $850 million. The agency received another $150 million in operating capital from the World Bank.

Projects supported by MIGA have widespread benefits: local jobs are created, tax revenue is generated, skills and technological know-how are transferred. Local communities often receive significant secondary benefits through improved infrastructure, including roads, electricity, hospitals, schools, and clean water. Foreign direct investment supported by MIGA also encourages similar local investments and spurs the growth of local businesses that supply related goods and services. As a result, developing countries have a greater chance to break the cycle of poverty.

MIGA's guarantee coverage requires investors to adhere to social and environmental standards that are considered to be the world's best. Without World Bank Group involvement, projects often go ahead without adequate safeguards.

MIGA both supports and draws on the extensive resources of the World Bank Group, applying unparalleled knowledge of emerging economies to the projects it guarantees. MIGA's unique strengths also derive from its structure as an international organization that acts as an umbrella of deterrence against government actions that could disrupt investments, and allows it to influence the resolution of potential disputes. MIGA's capacity to serve as an objective intermediary enhances investor confidence that an investment going into an emerging economy will be protected against non-commercial risks.

Concerns about uncertain political environments and perceptions of political risk often inhibit investment, with foreign direct investment (FDI) often going to a handful of countries and leaving the world's poorest economies largely ignored. MIGA is an important catalyst, increasingly promoting FDI — a key driver of growth — into developing countries through its guarantees, technical assistance, and legal services.

Since its inception, MIGA has issued more than 500 guarantees for projects in 78 developing countries. As of June 2001, total coverage issued exceeded $9 billion, bringing the estimated amount of foreign direct investment facilitated since inception to more than $41

U.S. Department of Commerce, International Trade Administration

Sub-Saharan African Member Countries of the Multilateral Investment Guarantee Agency

Member Countries (25):

Angola, Benin, Botswana, Burkina Faso, Cameroon, Congo (Democratic Republic of), Congo (Republic of), Ethiopia, Gambia, Ghana, Guinea, Ivory Coast, Kenya, Malawi, Mauritania, Mozambique, Namibia, Nigeria, Senegal, South Africa, Tanzania, Togo, Uganda, Zambia, Zimbabwe

Countries in the process of fulfilling membership requirements (3):

Gabon, Guinea-Bissau, Niger

Source: Multilateral Investment Guarantee Agency.

billion. The agency mobilized an additional $153 million in investment coverage in fiscal 2001 through its Cooperative Underwriting Program (CUP), encouraging private sector insurers into transactions they would not have otherwise undertaken, and helping the agency serve more clients.

MIGA's technical assistance services also play an integral role in catalyzing foreign direct investment by helping developing countries around the world define and implement strategies to promote investment. MIGA develops and deploys tools and technologies to support the spread of information on investment opportunities. Thousands of users of take advantage of MIGA's suite of on-line investment information services, which complement country-based capacity-building work.

The agency uses its legal services to further smooth possible impediments to investment. Through its dispute mediation program, MIGA helps governments and investors resolve their differences, and ultimately improve the country's investment climate.

MIGA complements the activities of other investment insurers and works with partners through its coinsurance and reinsurance programs to expand the capacity of the political risk insurance industry's income. To date, MIGA has officially established 18 such partnerships.

69

APPENDIX C: OVERSEAS PRIVATE INVESTMENT CORPORATION

The Overseas Private Investment Corporation is a self-sustaining federal agency whose purpose is to promote economic growth in developing countries by encouraging U.S. private investment in those nations. The Overseas Private Investment Corporation (OPIC) was established as an independent agency by the Foreign Affairs Reform and Restructuring Act of 1998 (112 Stat. 2681-790). OPIC assists American investors in four principal ways:

• financing of businesses through loans and loan guaranties;

• supporting private investment funds which provide equity for U.S. companies investing in projects overseas;

• insuring investments against a broad range of political risks; and

• engaging in outreach activities.

All of these programs are designed to reduce the perceived stumbling blocks and risks associated with overseas investment.

Organized as a corporation and structured to be responsive to private business, OPIC is mandated to mobilize and facilitate the participation of U.S. private capital and skills in the economic and social development of developing countries and emerging economies. Currently, OPIC programs are available for new business enterprises or expansion in some 140 countries worldwide. The corporation encourages American overseas private investment in sound business projects, thereby improving U.S. global competitiveness, creating American jobs, and increasing U.S. exports. The corporation does not support projects that will result in the loss of domestic jobs or have a negative impact on the host country's environment or workers' rights.

The corporation is governed by a 15-member board of directors, of whom eight are appointed from the private sector and seven from the federal government.

Activities

By reducing or eliminating certain perceived political risks for investors and providing financing and assistance not otherwise available, the corporation helps to reduce the unusual risks and problems that can make investment opportunities in the developing areas less attractive than in advanced countries. At the same time, it reduces the need for government-to-government assistance by involving the U.S. private sector in establishing capital-generation and strengthening private-sector economies in developing countries.

The corporation insures U.S. investors against the political risks of expropriation, inconvertibility of local currency earnings, and damage from war, revolution, insurrection, or civil strife. It also offers a special insurance policy to U.S. contractors and exporters against arbitrary drawings of letters of credit posted as bid, performance, or advance payment guaranties. Other special programs are offered for minerals exploration, oil and gas exploration, and development and leasing operations.

The corporation offers U.S. lenders protection against both commercial and political risks by guaranteeing payment of principal and interest on loans (up to $200 million) made to eligible private enterprises.

Its direct investment loans, offered to small and medium-sized businesses, generally cover terms of from 5 to 15 years and usually range from $2 million to $30 million with interest rates depending on assessment of the commercial risks of the project financed.

Additionally, OPIC supports a family of privately man-

Sub-Saharan Africa Country List for Programs of the Overseas Private Investment Corporation

Countries where OPIC programs are in full force (24):

Angola, Benin, Botswana, Burkina Faso, Cameroon, Congo (Democratic Republic of), Congo (Republic of), Ethiopia, Ghana, Guinea, Kenya, Malawi, Mauritania, Mozambique, Namibia, Niger, Nigeria, Senegal, South Africa, Tanzania, Togo, Uganda, Zambia, Zimbabwe

Countries where investment guaranty agreements are still in full force and efffective, but where OPIC programs are unilaterally inoperable for statutory, political, economic, or other reasons (3):

Ivory Coast, Gambia, Guinea-Bissau

Source: Overseas Private Investment Corporation.

---

aged direct investment funds in various regions and business sectors. Such funds currently operate in most countries in East Asia, sub-Saharan African, South America, Russia and other New Independent States, Poland, and other countries in Central Europe, India, and Israel.

Programs are available only for a new facility, expansion or modernization of an existing plant, or technological or service products designed to generate investment that will produce significant new benefits for host countries.

For further information, contact the Overseas Private Investment Corporation, 1100 New York Avenue N.W., Washington, DC 20527; stelephone (202) 336-8400; fax (202) 408-9859. Internet, *www.opic.gov.*

(Text from *U.S. Government Manual*, 2001–2001 edition.)

APPENDIX D: INTERNATIONAL FINANCE CORPORATION

The International Finance Corporation, part of the World Bank Group, fosters economic growth in the developing world by financing sustainable private sector investments, mobilizing capital in the international financial markets, and providing technical assistance to governments and business.

In partnership with private investors, IFC provides loan and equity finance for business ventures in developing countries and helps them stimulate the flow of savings and investment. IFC plays a catalytic role by demonstrating the profitability of investments in developing countries. And it further promotes economic development by working to build efficient capital markets.

Since its founding in 1956, IFC has committed more than $31 billion of its own funds and has arranged $20 billion in syndications for 2,636 companies in 140 developing countries. IFC coordinates its activities with the other institutions of the World Bank Group — the International Bank for Reconstruction and Development (IBRD or the World Bank), the International Development Association, and the Multilateral Investment Guarantee Agency — but is legally and financially independent. Its 175 member countries provide its share capital and collectively determine its policies.

Project Finance

IFC offers a full array of financial products and services to its client companies:

• long-term loans in major currencies, at fixed or variable rates

• equity investments

• quasi-equity instruments (subordinated loans, preferred stock, income notes)

• guarantees and standby financing

• risk management tools

To be eligible for IFC financing, projects must be profitable for investors, benefit the economy of the host country, and comply with stringent social and environmental guidelines. IFC finances projects in all types of industries, from infrastructure to financial services, from manufacturing to tourism. To ensure the participation of investors and lenders from the private sector, IFC limits the total amount of debt and equity financing it will provide for any single project to 25 percent of total estimated project costs; it may provide up to 35 percent of the equity capital for a project provided it is never the largest shareholder. IFC investments typically range from $1 million to $100 million.

Mobilization

Thanks to its record of success and special standing as a multilateral institution, IFC is able to act as a catalyst for private investment. Its participation in a project enhances investor confidence and attracts other lenders and shareholders. IFC mobilizes financing directly for sound companies in developing countries by syndicating loans with international commercial banks and underwriting investment funds and corporate securities issues; it also handles private placements of securities. For more information on IFC's syndications program, please visit *www.ifc.org/syndications*.

Advice and Technical Assistance

IFC advises businesses in developing countries on a wide variety of matters, including restructuring; the formulation of business plans; identification of markets, products, technologies, and financial and technical partners; and mobilization of project finance. It can

U.S. Department of Commerce, International Trade Administration

provide advisory services in the context of an investment, or independently for a fee, in line with market practice. For more information on IFC's donor-supported trust funds, please visit *www.ifc.org/taft*.

It also advises governments improving the environment for private investment, developing domestic capital markets, restructuring and privatizing state-owned enterprises, and attracting foreign direct investment. For more information on IFC's foreign investment advisory services, please visit *www.fias.net*.

Ownership and Management

IFC has 175 member countries. IFC's corporate powers are vested in its Board of Governors, to which member countries appoint representatives. IFC's share capital, which is paid in, is provided by its member countries, and voting is in proportion to the number of shares held. IFC's authorized capital is $2.45 billion.

The Board of Governors delegates many of its powers to a Board of Directors, composed of the executive directors of the IBRD, who represent IFC's member countries. The Board of Directors reviews all projects.

IFC is affiliated with the IBRD but has its own share capital, articles of agreement, and staff.

Funding of IFC's Activities

IFC's equity and quasi-equity investments are funded out of its net worth — the total of paid-in capital and retained earnings. Of the funding required for its lending operations, 80 percent is borrowed in the international financial markets through public bond issues or private placements; the remaining 20 percent is borrowed from the IBRD. IFC's bond issues have been given triple-A ratings by Moody's and Standard & Poor's.

For more information about the IFC, contact: Corporate Relations Unit, International Finance Corporation, 2121 Pennsylvania Avenue, N.W., Washington, DC 20433; telephone: (202) 473-3800; fax: (202) 974-4384; Internet: *www.ifc.org*.

www.ingramcontent.com/pod-product-compliance
Lightning Source LLC
Chambersburg PA
CBHW080432290526
45791CB00008BA/2468